The Search for the Golden Mission

A kid's fantastic journey of the 21 California missions

By Torrey Mahall
(A Fourth Grade Author)

Copyright © 2009 by Torrey Mahall
All rights reserved

Published by: Wayne MaHall
First edition, August 2009

ISBN 978-0-9827914-0-0

*This book is dedicated to
the 4th graders of California
who are passionate learners
and love to read*

Table of Contents

Introduction	i
The Journey Begins	1

Mission 1 – Mission San Diego de Alcala
    San Diego, CA   5
Mission 2 – Mission San Carlos Borromeo de Carmelo
    Carmel, CA   12
Mission 3 – Mission San Antonio de Padua
    Jolon, CA   18
Mission 4 – Mission San Gabriel Arcangel
    San Gabriel, CA   25
Mission 5 – Mission San Luis Obispo de Tolosa
    San Luis Obispo, CA   31
Mission 6 – Mission San Francisco de Asis
    San Francisco, CA   36
Mission 7 – Mission San Juan Capistrano
    San Juan Capistrano, CA   47
Mission 8 – Mission Santa Clara de Asis
    Santa Clara, CA   55
Mission 9 – Mission San Buenaventura
    Ventura, CA   64
Mission 10 – Mission Santa Barbara
    Santa Barbara, CA   70
Mission 11 – Mission La Purisima Concepcion
    Lompoc, CA   76
Mission 12 – Mission Santa Cruz
    Santa Cruz, CA   86
Mission 13 – Mission Nuestra Senora de la Soledad
    Soledad, CA   92
Mission 14 – Mission San Jose
    Fremont, CA   98
Mission 15 – Mission San Juan Bautista
    San Juan Bautista, CA   110

Mission 16 – Mission San Miguel Arcangel San Miguel, CA	116
Mission 17 – Mission San Fernando Rey de Espana San Fernando, CA	122
Mission 18 – Mission San Luis Rey de Francia Oceanside, CA	129
Mission 19 – Mission Santa Ines Solvang, CA	136
Mission 20 – Mission San Rafael Arcangel San Rafael, CA	144
Mission 21 – Mission San Francisco Solano Sonoma, CA	151
The Golden Mission Discovered	159

Saint Joseph's Day
    Mission San Juan Capistrano
        San Juan Capistrano, CA
	164

Appendix	168
Basilicas	169
El Camino Real	171
Father Junipero Serra	174
Stations of the Cross	176
Planning a Trip?	179
About the Author	191
Acknowledgements	192
Bibliography	193

Introduction

*H*i, I'm Torrey Mahall, a 4th grade public school student, and the author of this book. Before you start reading the book, there are a few things I want to tell you.

For my mission project, I decided to visit all 21 missions (from September to April), and write a book about them. My idea was to share with you the missions through the eyes of a 4th grader. Although the book is pretty much a tour of each mission, I wrote it around a mystery story to keep it from being too boring.

You don't have to read all the chapters if you don't want to, maybe just the missions you're interested in. However, I think you should read all of them, because each mission is unique.

The purpose of this book is to introduce and to motivate people to go to the missions. Hopefully, this book will convince you to go to one…or more. If you do go to more than one mission, I think it would be a great project to compare and contrast them.

You might wonder why the missions are listed the way they are. Well, this was the order they were founded in and it makes it easier for you to find them in the book. This is *not* the order we visited them in. And it's not the order you should visit them in either! (Imagine driving from San Diego all the way up to Carmel!) The characters did them in this order, because they could! That's the magic of writing!

After the chapter about the Saint Joseph's Day celebration at Mission San Juan Capistrano, I have written an appendix. The appendix is from my point of view. It covers Basilicas, El Camino Real, Father Junipero Serra, and Stations of the Cross. I also have a Planning a Trip section that will help you plan your mission journey.

I had an incredible time exploring the missions, and I hope you do too. Now take it away, Allison!

First: Mission San Fernando September 21, 2008

Last: Mission San Jose April 11, 2009

The Journey Begins

*H*i, my name is Allison. I am in 4th grade, and I am part of the CDA. CDA stands for Child Detective Agency. It is sometimes called Child Detective Association, but I like agency more. The CDA is a group of kids who all share an interest in solving somewhat complicated mysteries. I just recently solved a mystery about a missing key that someone accidentally threw in the recycling bin. It was a gruesome job, but someone had to do it.

Now I am going to introduce the craziest brother on the planet. He is my partner in the CDA. He can take annoying to extremes, play bad, bad, practical jokes, and nearly make you cry from his knock – knock jokes. He's Mark – my twin brother and personal noodlehead. I am just going to write that you would definitely not want to have him as a brother because he's a *noodlehead. Noodlehead.* If I could explain how much I don't care for him, this introduction would be thirty pages long. Sadly, he is my partner in this adventure. I guess that's just life.

During spring break, Mark and I heard about the Search for the Golden Mission. We decided to search the California missions to find it. Mishie (a small wingless fairy/tour guide) guided us through the missions, and we sort of ended up finding it, but I don't want to spoil the ending.

While we searched for the Golden Mission, we saw some really cool stuff. I wrote about my favorite things at the end of each chapter. They would make a great "I Spy" game when you tour the missions. Let the adventure begin!

One day, Mark and I were listening to the news because there was nothing better to do. I mean, almost all of Mark's old toy cars were crashed, every board game we owned was way too boring, and Mom banned us from playing baseball, soccer, badminton, or any other fun thing in the house because we broke her favorite lamp. Well, what else was there to do?

Mark and I are twins, but, in my opinion, we shouldn't be. Mark is the perfect kind of boy, who never gets involved in anything bad. He says I'm weird, weird, goofy, off–task, abnormal, unpredictable, and weird. Since we just solved our latest mystery, we have nothing to do now. Maybe we could find a good case watching the news.

Suddenly, the anchorman said, "Coming up next, there seems to be a rebellion at Derwood High. Can the teachers solve the problem? And, The Search for the Golden Mission seems to be going on once again. Michelle Brooks is live with the story. All of this, right after the break."

"Did you hear that?" Mark said, smiling.

"Yeah. Why are you so interested in high school kids being mean?"

"No, The Search of the Golden Mission thing! That could be our new mystery!"

"You thought the thing about the toilet plungers was a mystery."

Mark rolled his eyes at me, but we didn't talk anymore. The news was back on.

First they showed the thing about the high school rebellion. After a while the news anchorman said, "Interesting wasn't it? Now, we're going to hear about The Search for the Golden Mission, a famous hunt for a model made of gold. It is a priceless treasure, having been undiscovered for years! But now, clues have been revealed, showing the Golden Mission may be at one of the twenty-one California Missions. Here's Michelle Brooks with how it all happened."

"We don't need to hear that," said Mark, shutting off the TV. "Now we have a new mystery to solve."

I nodded. "Let's go."

We were almost to the door when Mark said, "Wait, how'll we get there?"

"Me," said a small, high–pitched voice. "I'll fly you guys there."

"Aaaaaahhhhhhh!" I screamed.

"Shut your mouth! Mom's going to hear you, and then we'll get in trouble, you don't want us to be grounded again, do

2

you, of course you know there's got to be a logical explanation for this, even though I can't think of one right now, oh my gosh, what in the world is that?" Mark said this all so fast, it was hard for me to make out what he was talking about. But, I looked up because I heard the last part: "What in the world is that?"

A little female person was hovering in front of us, barely the size of my hand. She looked like a fairy, with no wings. She had brunette hair; all tied up in a high ponytail, very white teeth, and was wearing a dress all shades of green, obviously, made of tree leaves. On one foot, she had a green shoe also made of leaves. I couldn't see if she had a shoe on the other foot because the skirt was long on that side. Around her neck she wore a black string, with a single charm on it, a golden bell.

"Hi," she said. "I'm Mishie. What're your names?"

"Mark," Mark said awkwardly.

"My name is Allison. Mark and I are part of the CDA, the Child Detective Agency. I was wondering if you could help us in any way. Right now, we're about to head off to the first mission in California, wherever that is. We're searching for that Golden Mission thing. We heard it on the news. Do you have any idea where it is, or how we can get there?"

Mark gave me a very-well-said-but-you-shouldn't-talk-to-strangers-so-easily-look. But, I didn't care. I was waiting for Mishie's reply.

"Yes, that's my job. I can fly you from mission to mission, and guide you along as you search. Just ask if you need any information."

"Okay," I said. "I think we should start now. What's the first mission?"

"Mission Basilica San Diego de Alcala. You can just call it Mission San Diego."

"Do you have anything else to tell us?" Mark asked.

"Yes," said Mishie. "About the flying. This is how it goes. If you guys are near me, you'll be able to fly, but only if I want you to. If I don't want you to, you won't be able to do it, even if *you* want to. Got that? Okay. One more thing. I already have our trip sort of planned. Your mom actually knows me, so if I leave a note saying where you guys went, it'll be okay. We'll do three missions a day, and have lunch...whenever we feel like it. Sound like a deal?"

"Yeah," Mark and I said in unison.

"Let's go." said Mishie, right after she wrote a note. It looked pretty funny because Mishie was, like, three inches shorter than the pencil.

We flew out the open door, and soon, I couldn't see the house. The three of us soared over houses and stores and schools and clinics and restaurants and apartments and public swimming pools. It was really awesome. I never believed people could fly without airplanes, or gliders, or something like that until now.

Mission One

Mission San Diego de Alcala
(Founded: 1769)

San Diego, CA

*Mother of the Missions

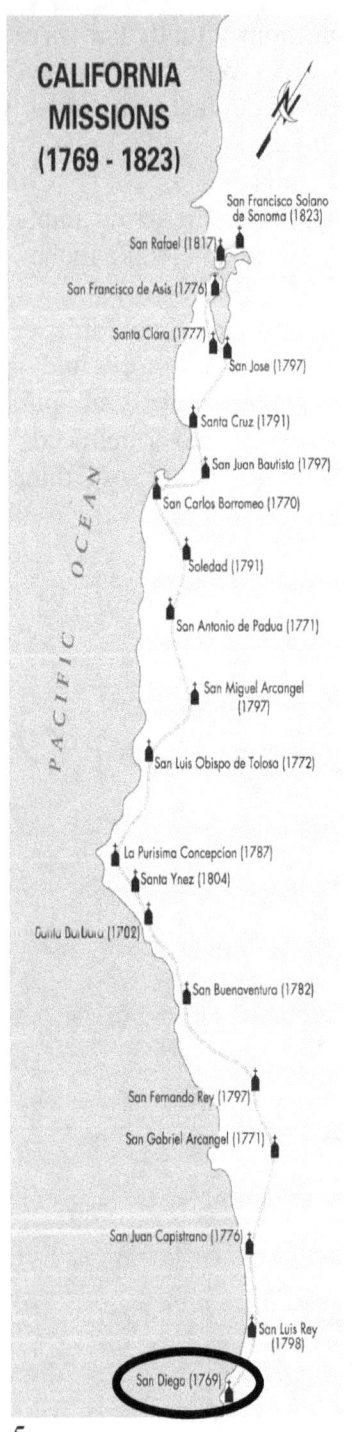

First Mission: Mission San Diego

*A*fter a short period of time, I looked down and saw a huge building with bells and all that stuff that makes a mission look like a mission.

"Land now," Mishie told us. Amazingly, I could land. And I never had any flying practice!

Before long, we were on the ground right in front of Mission San Diego. In front of us were 40 steps. Mark, Mishie and I raced to the top. Mishie won, of course, because she was flying, but I beat Mark.

Mishie pointed out that after 5 years of operation, in 1774, this mission was moved here. It was moved because this location was closer to Indian Villages, had a reliable source of water, and good farming land.

We went into the gift shop, which was the entrance to the mission.

When we were at the counter, the lady said, "$3.00 each please. If you want a tote–a–tape, that'd be $5.00."

"No," Mishie laughed. "Mishie service."

Whatever Mishie service is, it got us in for free. (No tax either!)

The lady smiled and told us we could enter. When we were outside, Mishie said the first place we should go was the Casa Del Padre Serra.

The Casa Del Padre Serra was the place where the priest (padre) of the mission lived. We got to go inside. There were two stories. On the first floor, there was a bed, a chair, a broom, and other items all crammed on one side of the room. The other side supplied nothing but a fireplace.

We were able to see the second floor from the first floor. To get up there, the priest would climb a rope ladder, and, before he slept, he would pull it up so bandits couldn't reach him.

Next, Mark, Mishie and I passed an archeological site. No one was there, but it looked as if they were halfway through digging up the *convento*, or friary. The friary was the place where the Franciscan missionaries lived while at the mission.

After that, the three of us walked down a hall with a big statue at the end. Next to the statue we noticed the fourteen Stations of the Cross. But, the pictures weren't painted. They were tile mosaics. I really liked them because they were colorful and looked a bit like stick figures.

The next place we went was the museum. The first display showed Indian tools and pots. The next one showed Indians' baskets. Farther down there was a mission bell. There was also a key, and lock, a plow, and horseshoe, a saw blade, and a door hinge that all belonged to Indians. In the next room there were framed models of all 21 missions glued to the wall. I liked looking at them because I saw the missions we'd be going to, and the one that we're at. I knew I might not see *all* of the missions, though, because we'd stop looking when we found the Golden Mission. There was also an original American flag, with thirteen stars representing the thirteen colonies.

When we had left the museum, we went into a chapel. It was like a small church. There were approximately 24 choir stalls in the chapel, all along the sides. It smelled musty, so Mark decided to be annoying and said, "Eww! I just realized that Allison didn't take a bath since last week! Now she stinks!"

"NO! It's you! Plus, I took a shower this morning!"
"Right," Mark rolled his eyes.
"I did!"
"I don't remember that…"
"I know why! Because you have a bad memory!"
"Who wins all the 'Memory' card games?"
"That's just your luck!"
"I see…" Mark rolled his eyes again.

I was about to say he was a noodlehead, and then I felt a small pinch on my arm.

"Come on, we're going someplace else." Mishie said.

Outside, Mark, Mishie and I looked at a stove Indians used for cooking. It was shaped like a dome and had a square hole where the food could go into. There were also some tools outside of the stove used for grinding, mashing, and other things.

Afterward, our trio visited the fountain. There were no fish, but there were lots of pennies, nickels, dimes, and algae. The algae were kind of gross, but the fountain was still very nice.

Mark ran ahead of us to the garden. He said he was just really eager to see the plants, but I knew he just wanted to be noodleheadish. We strolled along the path, and looked at some beautiful brick crosses. We also stopped at the Saint Francis Wishing well. Mark and I made a wish. I wished that Mark would stop being so annoying! After we had done all this, we looked at the beautiful bell tower. It had five bells. Mishie said that some people say that two of the bells are original, and others claim that four are. Mark said another word for the bell tower was campanario (Camp–uhn–air–ee–oh).

Next, the three of us wandered into the church. Over the thing that the priest stood in to give his sermon, there was something that looked like a combination between a canopy and an umbrella. I was wondering what it was.

"What's that?" I whispered.

"It signifies that this mission is a basilica," said Mark. "Only three other missions are basilicas: Mission Dolores in San Francisco, Mission Carlos Borromeo in Carmel, and Mission San Juan Capistrano in San Juan Capistrano. And by the way, the thing that the priest stands in is a *pulpit*." Mark rolled his eyes at me like I was the dumbest person in the world, which I wasn't. I already knew about the pulpit…sort of. Well, not really. Mark knows everything (unfortunately).

"How did you know?" I asked.

"Brains," he said. "Something you need."

After that, we strolled around the church some more. We saw the Fourteen Stations of the Cross, and looked at all of the statues on the altar. In our guide, it says that some Padres (priests) are buried up there, including Padre Jayme, a priest attacked by the Indians that invaded this mission. It's said that this is the only mission ever to be attacked by Indians, and this was the first church in California. There are square plaques each bearing the name of a priest. They are formed in the shape of a cross.

Farther down there was a replica of the original baptismal, a confessional, some candles and holy water. We decided that we were done touring the church, so we told Mishie we were ready to leave.

"Not yet," said Mishie. "I want to see if you can help the archeologists."

So Mishie had us go back to the archeological site. She asked if we could help and the people there said yes! So Mark and I got these shovel thingies and whisk brooms and we helped the archeologists dig. I really liked doing it because I thought it was a great way to look for the Golden Mission. We didn't find anything, but it was still pretty fun (excluding the part where Mark "accidentally" threw dirt in my face).

When Mishie said it was time we should leave, we said goodbye to the archeologists, and stood outside the entrance to the mission. There, I noticed nine interesting statues. Mishie pointed out that they all were of a Patron Saint and its mission. She said that these were of the first nine missions that Father Junipero Serra founded.

After a long silence, Mishie said, "All right, guys. Time to go."

Mark and I nodded.

We walked down the 40 steps, Mishie smiled, my feet lifted off the ground, and we were in the air once again. We didn't find the Golden Mission, but who would expect to find something on your first try? Now, we were off to the next mission, Mission San Carlos Borromeo.

"Hey!" I shouted as we were flying to the next mission. "There's a Coco's. I'm hungry; let's eat there."

"Okay," said Mishie.

Mark held up three fingers: his pointer, his middle, and his fourth finger, all at the same time. Then he made an L sign with this pointer and his thumb.

"What does that mean?" I asked.

"Whatever, loser," he said.

"I guess you mean yes…" If you don't understand Mark, just pretend he is agreeing with you.

We went down to the Coco's, and I got macaroni and cheese. I didn't pay attention to Mark (why would I? He's boring), so I don't know what he got. After a very good meal, we left, and I don't know how Mishie paid, but she did. This is cool. I mean, Mishie pays for everything, and I don't have to do a thing. We walked a little further, and then we flew off and continued to make our way to the next mission.

Favorite Things at Mission San Diego

1. When the tour was finished, I got to help the **archeologists** try to **uncover artifacts**. You should really volunteer if they let you.
2. In front of the mission, there were **Patron Saint statues**. They were holding buildings that Mishie said were missions. I really like them.
3. Outside, in the garden, near the bell tower, there were these really neat **brick crosses** that had **leis** and other items similar to necklaces strung around them. Those crosses were really pretty.
4. Inside the museum, there were twenty-one **framed models** of the missions. Mishie pointed out the missions we'd be going to today, which made them extra special.
5. When I had almost left, I heard the sound of **bells**. I walked to the bell tower, and saw someone **ringing** them. The sound was loud, but wonderful. If possible, take time to listen to the bells.
6. In a hallway, there were the 14 **Station of the Cross**. But, they were **tile mosaics**, not paintings. The thing I liked about the tile mosaics was that they told the story of Jesus, without being bloody and frightening.

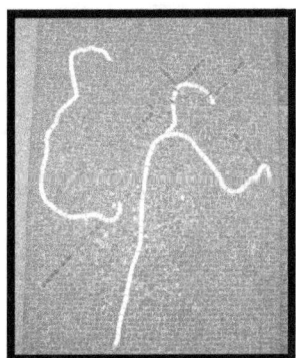

Mission Two

Mission San Carlos Borromeo de Carmelo

(Founded: 1770)

Carmel, CA

*Father of the Missions

CALIFORNIA MISSIONS (1769 - 1823)

- San Francisco Solano de Sonoma (1823)
- San Rafael (1817)
- San Francisco de Asis (1776)
- Santa Clara (1777)
- San Jose (1797)
- Santa Cruz (1791)
- San Juan Bautista (1797)
- San Carlos Borromeo (1770)
- Soledad (1791)
- San Antonio de Padua (1771)
- San Miguel Arcangel (1797)
- San Luis Obispo de Tolosa (1772)
- La Purisima Concepcion (1787)
- Santa Ynez (1804)
- Santa Barbara (1782)
- San Buenaventura (1782)
- San Fernando Rey (1797)
- San Gabriel Arcangel (1771)
- San Juan Capistrano (1776)
- San Luis Rey (1798)
- San Diego (1769)

Second Mission: Mission San Carlos

*A*fter flying for…a long time, maybe 10 minutes, we finally arrived at Mission San Carlos. I pointed out to Mishie that it had taken *forever* to get there, but she said it would have been hours longer if we had gotten there by car.

Mishie flew us downward and we landed with a small 'thump.'

"Here we are," Mishie's grin nearly reached her pointed ears. "Our second mission."

Then, I heard a loud CRACK! Was it a storm? Was it Mark breaking his arm? (Hopefully!) Or was it Santa Claus cracking his whip on the reindeer? If you went with the storm, you were right. It started to rain.

Detectives are always ready. Mark and I pulled out our umbrellas and hoisted them over our heads. Mishie pulled out a little paper umbrella that you get at a Chinese restaurant and used it to protect her. And it worked!

We went inside the building to pay. "Mishie service," said Mishie.

We walked into the cemetery, and were surprised at the many abalone shells set on top of the graves. They were really sparkly and awesome. Mishie said that they weren't really there for a mission-related reason; they were just decorations.

Since it was raining, Mishie said we should do an indoor activity, which is exactly what we did. We went inside the Mora Chapel Museum. In the center of the room was the Serra sarcophagus, a piece of art shaped like a coffin that had statues around it. The statues were praying and kneeling around the coffin with Father Serra on top of it. There was nothing in the coffin; it was just a piece of artwork.

I started walking around the sarcophagus. I was looking for clues. Since Mark *is* my partner, I decided to ask him if he found anything. "Mark, did you…Mark?"

Mark was gone! I thought I should celebrate, but then I realized maybe it wasn't so good. I would be in a lot of trouble once I came home and had to tell Mom I lost my brother. So I stopped being happy and looked for him.

The last time I saw him, he was somewhere around the Serra sarcophagus. So I looked behind the sarcophagus, and…

"BOO!"

"Aaaaaaaaaaaahhhhhhhhh!"

"I scared you, I scared you!" Mark chanted.

"Did not!"

"Whatever," Mark said.

Mishie came over to us and said, "Oooh, look at those paintings," so we would stop arguing.

On the walls and in glass cases, there were beautiful paintings of every mission. There were more than twenty-one, though. Some were satellites (offshoots) of the main missions, and some weren't even California missions. I saw some from New Mexico, and some from Arizona.

Next, the three of us scurried to the church. We knew this mission was a basilica by the umbrella–canopy thing inside the church, and of course; there were also the Fourteen Stations of the Cross. In another room in the church, there was a plaque on the floor, but I don't remember what it said.

When I first looked at the altar I saw a very bloody statue of Jesus on the cross, it frightened me, so I didn't look at the altar anymore. Instead, we looked at the grave of Father Junipero Serra, the man who founded the first nine missions. That's right; he was buried in the mission church. He apparently died at Mission San Carlos, so it seemed appropriate to bury him here. People believe that this was also Father Serra's favorite mission, so that's another reason why it's appropriate. When we were finally leaving the church, I saw a really neat organ in the rear balcony looking over the church. It was really awesome, and we stared at it for I don't know how long.

After a long while, Mark, Mishie and I took a walk in the garden. We looked at the bell tower of this mission, and Mishie said that it held 8 bells. Wow! And most of them are original. We passed some really beautiful plants and statues that you'll just have to see, and in a little bit, we ended up in a building dedicated to Harry Downie, who was the main restorer of the mission.

That building was a museum. In one glass case, there were things used to build the mission, like nails and stones (the church was made out of stone).

In the next room, there was a model of Mission San Carlos made by Harry when he was only 12. And it was a really good model; it looked like a professional made it! There was also another model of a mission that Mishie said looked like the mission in San Juan Bautista, a mission we haven't visited yet. Then we went back to the first room, and saw the original cross that used to be on the church.

Our trio went through the cemetery again and found that Harry Downie was buried there. That's pretty special.

After that, we visited the Munras Museum. My favorite thing about the first room was the windows. They had that old–fashioned wavy glass that is kind of hard to see through. There was also a circle design on the window. I loved it! In the first glass case, there was a saddle used for riding horses. In another there were fans, and in one more, there was jewelry. The last cabinet was dedicated to Indians, and it had that grinder thing, some shell necklaces, and a book containing cures for sicknesses. I saw a cure for the hiccups but I forgot what it was. There was also the Munras family tree.

Mishie showed us into the second room, but there wasn't much to see. It was just a display of the living room, and the Golden Mission *definitely* wouldn't be there.

It was still raining, but Mishie said we had to still do some outside activities. So we walked around the mission school. They taught grades kindergarten through 8th grade. We looked inside the classrooms, but didn't find anything.

Next, we went into the courtyard, where there was a fountain and a really neat angel sculpture. (Look at <u>Favorite Things</u> for details.)

Shortly after, Mark, Mishie and I went inside the last museum. They had a wagon, a confessional, and a big pot inside there. There was also a glass case dedicated to music. It had violins and music sheets.

The library had crucifixes that were scary to me. It also had books. Mark liked the books. (☺) On the way out, Mishie said it was the oldest library in California. I thought this was interesting, and Mark must have too, because he took 2 pages of notes on it.

Afterward, we saw a display of what a kitchen might have looked like, and another display of the dining room. We looked at china bowls and plates in glass cases.

The last room was Father Serra's bedroom. It had a bed, a trunk (or chest, however you want to put it), and a desk. This was the room he died in. We were just walking out of the hall when we saw a map. It was really neat, and Mishie showed us which mission we were going to next.

"We're done," Mishie said. "Ready?"

Mark and I nodded.

"We didn't find any clues, though," said Mark.

"That's OK." Mishie assured us. "I'm sure you'll find it."

I was quiet for a while. I wondered if we really would. This was only our second mission, but who would be lucky enough to find something so early? Still, you would expect to find at least a clue, right? No clues. No leads, no lost leads…

"Don't just stand there, Allison! We need to go; come on!" Mark said.

"Sheesh! You don't have to be so bossy and demanding and…noodleheadish."

Mishie heaved us up in the air and we were off.

16

Favorite Things at Mission San Carlos

1. All of the **graves** in the cemetery had at least three **abalone shells** on them. They were sparkling in the rain, and I thought they were really pretty. But they were only for decoration, not for any mission-related purpose.
2. Inside the **Munras Museum**, there was a **wavy window** that had a circle design on it. It was super cool. You've got to see this.
3. When we were exiting the church, there was a **pipe organ** in the rear balcony that looked awesome. It had a bunch of different colors painted on it, and… well…it just looked amazing.
4. The front **church window** was really neat, too. It was kind of off center, and it had a really cool shape, like a star with lots of points.

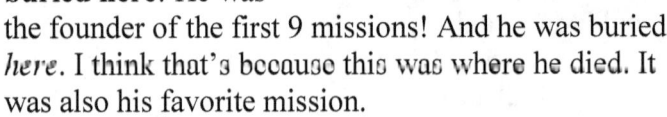

5. **Father Serra is buried here**! He was the founder of the first 9 missions! And he was buried *here*. I think that's because this was where he died. It was also his favorite mission.
6. When we had finished walking around the school, we went in the courtyard that was close, and there was a really neat **sculpture** of an **angel** there. It was modern and colorful.

Mission Three

Mission San Antonio de Padua

(Founded: 1771)

Jolon, CA

Mission of the Sierras

Also known as:
*The Mission that Time Forgot

Third Mission: Mission San Antonio

After flying some, we soon arrived at Mission San Antonio. I was surprised at the location of the mission. It was practically in the middle of nowhere. I mean, it wasn't deserted, but it was pretty far away from everything else. The only signs of people were the army guys at the military base we had to fly over.

We landed in front of the mission. The first thing I saw was an adorable kitten sitting on the front steps. It had black fur all over, and light green eyes. I wanted to take it home with me, but that probably wasn't allowed.

Since Mission San Antonio was in the center of . . . nothing, Mark decided we should go out and read every sign that was posted in the dead grass. He is so weird.

Before we went out to read the boring, not-going-to-help-us-find-the-Golden-Mission signs, Mark started talking to Mishie about something uninteresting, probably the history of Mission San Antonio. I realized that this was a good opportunity to daydream.

I looked at the mission. It was really different from the other two I've been to. I mean, it was out in the middle of nowhere. San Diego and San Carlos were in the middle of cities. It was so easy for me to imagine that I was back in the days when this was still a thriving mission…

Mark pulled on my arm really hard, which messed up my daydreaming. "Come on! We need to read the signs!" he said. I just gave him an evil look because I didn't feel like arguing right now.

One sign told about an Indian sweat–house. There was just a ditch where the sweat–house used to be, so we looked in the big hole, but didn't find the Golden Mission. Another was about the Salinan Tribe, the Indian tribe of this mission. A bit farther down, there was a well and a reservoir. A sign told about that, too. It said that the reservoir used to be 14' long, and then it was extended to 37'. It had a 15,000 gallon capacity. Two men operating the pump of the well could fill up the reservoir in 2 hours. The fourth sign said that the mission was made out of adobe bricks. The bricks were usually 11" by 23" by 4". They weighed about 60 pounds each. My favorite sign told how many sheep used to be at the mission in 1826. 11,000! Also, there was a gigantic concrete block that had the cattle mark of the mission on it. It was an A with a swirly thing coming out the side. (I didn't describe that very well; you'll see it if you go there.)

    We saw a lot more material before going into the mission. For instance, all three of us checked out the El Camino Real bell, a cross in memory of Father Junipero Serra, an old olive crusher, and an Indian hut (kiicha). The awesome thing about the hut was that part of the dried grass that covered it up had fallen off, so you could see through one half of the hut. We also saw the Indian Cemetery. At first, I had no idea how this empty space, with adobe around it, could be a cemetery. There were no gravestones, plaques or flowers. It was simply bare ground. I soon learned that the Indians did not want gravestone markers or plaques, or any of that kind of stuff for some reason.

    Some other things we looked at included the remains of the house of the mayordomo, which was just a few pieces of adobe. In case you're wondering, the mayordomo is, basically, the overseer of the mission. He was in charge of the work and supervised the Indians' performance of duties.

    Mark, Mishie and I looked at a house that had a dried-up creek underneath it, and then we looked at the *original* mission well.

    After a long time outside, we finally came inside the gift shop to start our tour.

    Up at the front desk, the clerk told us how much we had to pay. She didn't notice Mishie. Mishie had to clear her throat and almost yell, "MISHIE SERVICE!" for her to hear her.

    Before we left, I asked the clerk how many kitties there were, and what their names were. I got an answer. There were three cats. The biggest one was named Rosario. She couldn't remember the middle one's name, but the youngest and smallest was Baby.

Shortly, we had entered the museum. We looked at a lot of models and displays. My favorite display was one of a blindfolded burro hauling an olive crusher to mash the olives. In one room, there was a weaving loom. In another, candles were hanging from the ceiling, drying.

I liked the music room a lot. There was a giant painting of a hand on the wall. Different numbers and letters were on the hand in different places. Mark told me that when someone was conducting a band, they would point to a place on their hand, and the band would play a certain note.

There were also other things in the room, such as instruments. I saw a harp, some drums, flutes, a violin, and lots of other stuff, too.

As we were leaving, Mark pointed to the bottom of his palm.

"What's that supposed to mean?" I asked him, since the entire bottom of the hand in the painting was blank.

Mark took a blue pen that said "CDA: Child Detective Agency" on it, and wrote something on his hand.

He turned his hand around and pointed to where some words were. The words were: "Hi, Allison! You are a stupid sister."

"You better wash that off by the end of today," I whispered as we went into the next room of the museum.

Next, we went in the original wine vat. There were two stairways. Eventually, Mark, Mishie, and I went down and up both. Up the up one, we spotted a very deep wine vat. I would say it's 15 feet deep or more. Mishie said that the grapes were crushed in the vat, and then the juice flowed through the open drain to the barrels in the cellar. Down the down one, there were the barrels that Mishie talked about.

We exited the wine vat and cellar and looked through glass windows to see the places where Padres stayed.

After walking through more displays, we exited the museum. We then went to the courtyard. Beautiful trees, plants, bushes, and cats were everywhere. I saw three kitties.

Two were gathered under a tree, and one was near a rosebush. They all looked exactly the same.

I continued my tour of the mission. I went under a grape vine that had grapes from the original stock cultivated in the vineyard of the mission. There was also a fountain.

Then, we went inside the church. Mark, Mishie, and I looked at the Fourteen Stations of the Cross, and admired the simple altar. I also really liked the ceiling because it was a really cool shape. It was flat in the middle, but had about 45 degree angles on both sides, like the top of a hexagon. I also thought the ceiling was really unique because it wasn't painted at all; it was just the bare wood. There was also a strange painting that had a skeleton in it. Mark read the sign about it and he said that the painting was done in Mexico by an unknown artist. It's a copy of an original done by Jean Cousin le Jeune for a church in France in 1812. Paintings like these were used by the Padres primarily as teaching aides. What I liked most about the church was the organ in there.

We strolled a little more through the mission and then decided to go outside and look at more signs. We were just about ready to step onto the dirt when Mishie said, "Hang on a moment!"

I stopped. "What?"

"Turn around."

"Okay…"

"See the bell in the middle niche of the campanario? Remember, a campanario is a bell tower."

"Yes, I see it."

"Well," said Mishie in her listen-I'm-going-to-give-you-some-information-now voice, "that bell was cast especially for this mission, and it is the first mission bell made in California. It is 24 inches in diameter and weighs 500 pounds."

"Interesting," I said.

"Yeah," Mark said. Then he took 5 pages of notes on the bell.

After that, we saw the remains of the pottery and tile shop, the Indians' bathing and washing pool, and a rip saw. I also saw a California redwood tree, a pomegranate tree preserved from the mission days, and a gigantic olive tree. Mark said that the olive tree was planted by the Padres about 1836, so that's why it is so big.

We saw beehive ovens throughout this area, and Mark said, "Hey, Allison! This sign says beehive ovens were built of adobe, and were used for baking bread. Charcoal was used to heat them up."

I didn't feel like talking to Mark after he ruined 5 pages of our notepad. I could have used those pages for something that would actually help us. "I don't care!" I yelled at him.

He shrugged, and then began writing more notes.

"NO!" I shouted as I grabbed the notepad from his hands.

"What?"

"Don't ruin our notepad! I could use it for something useful, like writing hiding places for the Golden Mission! You don't have to read all these signs and take all these notes! Were only here to search, Mark, not to…to read signs! And really, it's not going to help! I mean, who cares about beehive ovens and charcoal and baking bread…and…and… whatever! It's not going to help! It's meaningless! You don't have to read a sign every time you see one! It's not like it leads us to clues or…"

"Hey, look! A clue on the sign!"

"What?"

"Just kidding!"

The last thing we did was come back to the mission to see if we missed anything. We did. In the front, there was a sign that said that the first marriage in California took place at this mission. It was between Juan Mariu Ruiz and Margarita de Cortona. It took place on May 16, 1773.

This was the end of our tour. In a few minutes, Mishie had led us out of the mission, and we were on our way to the hotel. The first day of missions, I thought, was fun! I was looking forward to tomorrow.

Favorite Things at Mission San Antonio

1. When we were walking through the mission, I noticed that there were adorable **kittens** walking throughout the mission, too. All were black, with green eyes. I adored the kitties walking around.
2. A sign at the mission told Mark, Mishie and I that the **first marriage** in California took place right here, at this mission. I found that pretty interesting.
3. As I said before, Mission San Antonio was located right inside a **military base**. I got a picture next to a gigantic tank that was there.
4. In the museum, there was a **model of an olive crusher**. A blindfolded mule or burro pulled a big stone wheel, and this squashed the olives.
5. Before entering the actual mission, we saw a display of what an Indian hut (**kiicha**) might have looked like when the mission still had Indians at it.
6. In the music room, there was a big **picture of a hand** on the wall. The conductor would point to a place on his hand so the orchestra would know which note to play. Each place on his hand meant a certain note for them to play.

Note: Around Thanksgiving, there will be decorations all over the mission for the "Evening in the Garden" celebration. They are really pretty.

Mission Four

Mission San Gabriel, Arcangel
(Founded: 1771)

San Gabriel, CA

Pride of the Missions

Also known as:
* Mother of Agriculture in California

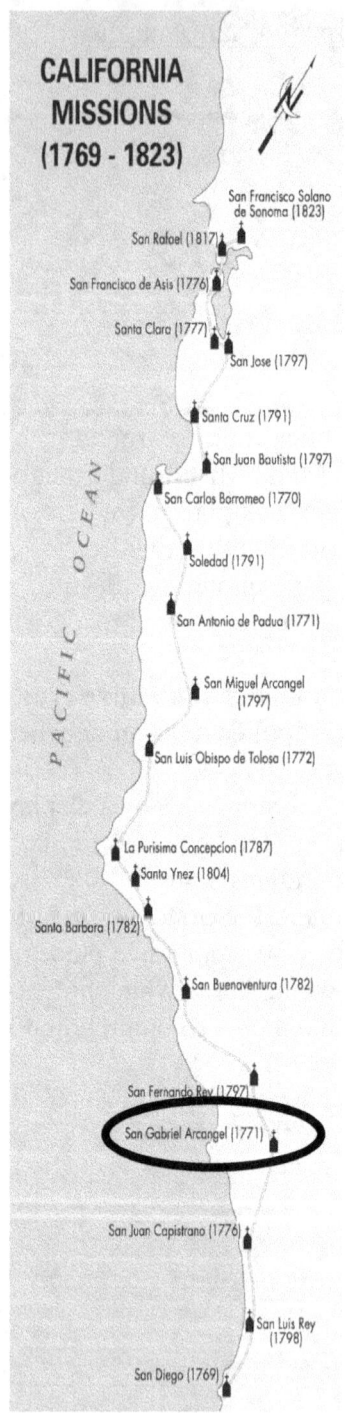

Fourth Mission: Mission San Gabriel

*W*e landed on the ground again. I think I'm getting used to this flying stuff. We were right in front of Mission San Gabriel, Pride of the Missions. Here, the gift shop was the entrance.

We walked into the gift shop, and the clerk told us how much we had to pay. Of course, we didn't have to pay anything because Mishie bowed low, and said, "Mishie service," and we were all let in for free.

When we walked out the door, we found ourselves in the Peace Garden. The first thing I saw was a fountain. It must have been the first thing Mark saw too, because he ran to the fountain instantly. We both decided to see what the water felt like. Mark pushed me a bit to put his hand in. My hat slid over my eyes.

"Watch it!" I yelled.

"Sorry," said Mark and nudged me some more.

This time, my hat fell in the water. I glared at Mark.

"Thanks," I said sarcastically.

"You're welcome," said Mark, throwing the soggy hat onto my head. Now my hair was wet as well as my hat. Mark's a great guy to have around if you'd like to be annoyed.

Mishie had persuaded us into moving farther into the garden. She had us sit down on a bench, and then she persuaded us into actually *apologizing* to each other. WOW!

If you walk further, a gate should be open. The gate leads to a place where they have a model of each mission. The models were made by Claretian missionaries in 1932. They were restored by the Girl Scouts in 2007. I looked at every mission carefully, looking for clues. Mark took notes and wrote every possible hiding place for the Golden Mission. His notes took up about three pages of the tiny notebook we share. I'm pretty involved in the mystery, but he's obsessed with this.

I spotted an anchor that was used on a ship that brought goods to the missions. But, we didn't find any clues there.

When we had returned from looking at the anchor, the three of us went inside an old kitchen. There were pots and pans everywhere, and there was a table. I enjoyed seeing it.

We walked past a deep rectangular hole that we couldn't check out because we had to stay on schedule, and soon arrived at a place with some tallow vats. They were really deep holes that became narrower and narrower the farther down you go. I took a picture right over one. It looked like the tallow vat was going to suck me up.

"Just in case you don't know," said Mishie, "tallow was a product made of animal fat that was used in candles, grease, ointment and even soap."

I giggled. "Animal fat soap!" I whispered to Mark.

He gave me the Allison-that's-so-immature look.

I stuck my tongue out at him.

Soon, we had arrived at the aqueduct. There was part of an old pipe sticking out of some brick. There was also a huge pot that looked like a cauldron. I didn't read the sign, so I'm not completely sure what it's for. (Mark read the sign. Ask him.) There were also brick fireplaces that the "cauldrons" were over. They looked like horseshoes. I really liked that section of the mission.

Soon afterward, we looked at an ancient grape vine. The trunk of the tree was humongous and all twisted, and the branches went out for yards! Supposedly, it was there since 1826. Mishie said that this mission made wine for all of the other missions. Even though there were no clues, Mark, Mishie and I were all impressed.

After that, we visited the San Gabriel Mission Church. The architecture was stunning. A green light was coming in through the windows, and making some of the benches look as if they were painted green. Hanging on the ceiling was a small chandelier. There was a pattern of fish painted around it on the ceiling.

I looked at the altar and noticed something peculiar. The statues were partially hanging over the ledges! I asked Mishie why they were like that and she said, "The altar was brought here in pieces, and at the same time, the statues were ordered. Well, when they came it was figured out that they were too wide for the altar. So they're hanging over the ledges now."

"They would fall off really easily in an earthquake, wouldn't they?" I asked.

"Actually," said Mishie. "No. There's some wire wound around their waists that connects them to the altar, so they're pretty secure."

As soon as we had exited the church, I noticed the remains of something up against the wall of the church.

"What's that?" I asked Mishie.

"It's what's left of the original bell tower. In the earthquake of 1812, it was destroyed."

Mark, Mishie and I went into the cemetery. There are supposed to be 200 people buried in Mission San Gabriel. But, they're not all in the cemetery. After a while, we found the grave of Antonio, the first Indian buried at this cemetery. He died October 20, 1778.

Next to the cemetery was a long grape arbor that I walked under. Mishie called it the famous grapevine walkway.

After walking a bit, we all decided to go into another building. Mishie let me ring the mission bell. But, Mark got to do it, too, which sucked. Then, we went into another room where there were a few drawers, a mirror, and a golden cross. The chest of drawers was really big, and Mishie said that it was made without any nails! I didn't think that was possible, because it seemed really hard, but I believed her anyway. Next, we visited a room that showed tools used to make wine. The winery, obviously.

There was a door outside of the building. The door was really big, but there was a smaller door inside it. The sign said that on Monday through Saturday, the small door was used. On Sunday, the larger door was used.

Next, Mark, Mishie and I entered a room with a bed, two chairs, and one piece if artwork on the wall. I forgot what this room was for, so if you go to Mission San Gabriel, please look at a sign or something.

Then, we went into what I think was a music room. There was a piano, a guitar, and some pictures on the wall. I did not read the sign on this, either, so make sure you do. There were also these things that looked like choir stalls. I sat in one, but the things that I thought were armrests were way too high. They were about level with my shoulders.

Soon, we were heading for the exit of Mission San Gabriel. Mishie decided to start a conversation.

She said, "Did you guys find any clues?"

"Yes," I said. "There are 21 possible hiding places for the Golden Mission here. The Golden Mission can be inside every one of those little models of the missions."

"Really?" asked Mark. "According to me, there are numerous hiding places. Your estimation is wrong."

"How many are there then, Brainiac?"

Mark sighed. "Ahhh, you wouldn't understand, my dumb sister," he said dramatically.

"Of course I would understand! I'm your twin! And I'm not *dumb*!"

"Ahhhh," Mark sighed dramatically again.

"Really, you need to stop acting out," I started. "Do you know how much I hate it when you start doing that? You remind me of those people that try to calm other people down. You know? And that weird 'Ahhh', it sounds like you're meditating. And I'm not dumb! You're just a nerd! Like all the other nerds who think they're so smart, but they're really not! Like all the other noodleheads! All the other noodleheads like you!"

"I hate it when you do monologues," Mark said.

"Let's fly," Mishie said.

Favorite Things at Mission San Gabriel

1. There was a really cool **drinking fountain** by the bathrooms. I advise you to try the water from the fountain. The water is good, and the fountain is fun!

2. The **models of the missions** are worth seeing. They're really awesome.

3. The **tallow vats** are super deep, and when you look down, you feel as if you're being sucked in. I loved them.

4. Right by the tallow vats, there are a bunch of **cacti**. I spotted one that looked like **Mickey Mouse**. It looked awesome!

5. In one building, there was a **bell** that the father might let you **ring** by pulling a rope. I got to ring it, and so did Mark. It made a great sound, and it was super cool.

6. Mark, Mishie and I walked under a **grape vine** that was *very* large. We stayed under it for a long time because of its awesomeness.

7. When we exited the place where we got to ring the bells, there was a **door** on display. It had a smaller door carved in it. The small door was used to enter the church on Monday through Saturday, and the big one was only used on Sunday.

8. A **green light** was pouring in from the window of the **church**. It made our clothes and skin look green. And it made Mishie's dress even greener.

9. There's a great **fountain** in the **Peace Garden**. Make sure you stop by that.

Mission Five

Mission San Luis Obispo de Tolosa

(Founded: 1772)

San Luis Obispo, CA

Mission in the Valley of Bears

Fifth Mission: Mission San Luis Obispo

*W*e zoomed down toward Mission San Luis Obispo, Mission in the Valley of Bears. It was called this because the area nearby had a lot of bears, which provided the mission with bear meat to save the people from starving. Once I found out about this information, the statue of bears outside the mission seemed appropriate. The bear statues were inside a fountain, along with another statue of an Indian boy. According to the sign, this statue was called Tuquski' Wa Suwa', which means Bear and Child. I really liked this statue/fountain thing.

We made a landing in front of the mission. Then, we peeked into the church. Some people were inside. But, not fathers or sisters or those kinds of people. They were builders. Not as if they were building the church, they were repairing statues, and archways and stuff. So, the church was off limits. Because of this, our tour was shorter than usual. Maybe when you go there, the church will be open. I hoped the builders wouldn't find the Golden Mission before us! And we couldn't see the altar carved by Harry Downie. (Harry Downie really carved the altar. I'm not kidding!)

Bonus Fact That Has Nothing To Do With What I Was Talking About Before: This is the only mission with an L shaped church. When we were flying over the mission, I noticed that the church was in an L shape.

When Mark, Mishie and I were going up the few steps leading to the church, Mark saw a sign that showed the different bells at the mission. He read all this boring, informative stuff on the sign that I didn't listen to. If you want to hear about it, look at the <u>Favorite Things</u> section and you'll see where Mark ordered me to write something about the bells.

Before we went inside the gift shop, I noticed that the mission church had pretty large doors. I asked Mishie why they were so big.

"Sometimes, people rode their horses into the church," she replied. "So the doors had to be big enough. Also, this portico..."

"What's a portico?" I asked.

"It's like a...um....I..."

Mark, the explainer, interrupted. "A portico is a walkway that has a roof over it. The roof is supported by columns. It's a lot like a patio."

"Thank you Mark," I said sarcastically. As you probably already know, I never really mean it when I thank my brother.

"Anyway," said Mishie, "This is the only mission with a portico."

When we were finally inside the gift shop, we got a map, Mishie said, "Mishie service," even though you only had to make a donation. Then, we went into the museum. They showed arrowheads, animal skins, Indian tools, baskets, and more. We also looked at pictures of the missions that dated back to the early 1900's. There was a lot of stuff in the museum, but if I wrote it all down, the list would probably go on for many pages. You'll have to visit the mission yourself.

Outside in the courtyard, there were many things I liked. They had the original bells from the bell tower on display, and really cool plants, like a tree that looked like an elephant's foot, a big curly thingy, and yellow roses. The original bells were called the Joy Bell, the Gloria Bell, and the Sorrow Bell. I made a wish above the wishing well, too. I mostly forgot what it was, but I remember that it had something to do with Mark and falling and a cliff. What I thought was really interesting was that a barbeque was outside. There was also a grape arbor.

A fountain was in another area along with a statue of what I think is a saint.

After peeking in the church one more time and searching in the courtyard a little more, Mark Mishie and I decided to leave. Since there was no cemetery, (this was the only mission without one) our tour/hunt was over. We stopped at the first restaurant we spotted, Subway, and had lunch there. We left for the next mission after that.

Favorite Things at Mission San Luis Obispo

1. Just outside the mission, there is a **fountain** with statue of a **bear**, its cubs, and an Indian child. I thought it was really cool.
2. Before we went inside the mission, I saw a sign that told about the **five mission bells**. Though you can only see three from the front, there are actually five bells. The other two are on the sides. Each bell is named after one of the first five California Missions. The first is named Diego (San Diego). The second is named Carlos (San Carlos). The third is named Antonio (San Antonio). The fourth is Gabriel (San Gabriel). The last one is Luis (San Luis Obispo).
3. The last thing I liked most about the mission was that there was an awesome **grape vine arbor** in the courtyard. I walked under it, and thought it was really neat.

Mission Six

Mission San Francisco de Asis
(Founded: 1776)

San Francisco, CA

* *Mission Dolores*

Sixth Mission: Mission San Francisco

I like touching the clouds. It's fun. They feel soft and fluffy, and they remind me of my pillow back home with a picture of a cute kitten on it. The kitten looks a lot like *my* kitten, Mr. Fwibble-Wibble. Mr. Fwibble-Wibble is a girl. (I know it's funny.)

Anyway, I was touching the clouds, and then I noticed I was starting to touch these really wet grayish ones. I looked down and it was raining. When I looked down I saw Mission San Francisco de Asis, more commonly known as Mission Dolores, so we landed, and we pulled out the umbrellas we used at Mission San Carlos Borromeo. The big ones for Mark and me, and the little purple paper one with really pretty flowers on it for Mishie.

"Whoa..." I said when we got to the mission. It was super tall, and it had really cool designs on the bell towers. Then I said, "Oh, my gosh... Wow..." This mission was so different! I've only been to five others, but they aren't this tall or this pretty.... Wow. It was so pretty, I was beginning to question if this even *was* the mission. But there was proof! The sign right there said "Mission Dolores" on it. I asked Mishie the question anyway, even though I knew the answer would be yes.

"Is this church...the mission?"

"No."

"What?" I was staring at Mishie like she was even more cuckoo than Mark. "But there's the sign, right there. It says, 'Mission Dolores.' This has got to be the mission! Are you okay?"

"I'm fine. I just need to explain some stuff to you."

I was thinking about saying, "Explain what? You can't doubt a sign." But I didn't say that. That would be too Mark-ish. I decided to listen to whatever Mishie said because she usually was right.

Mishie pointed to a small, white building that looked a lot more like a regular mission. "That is Mission San Francisco de Asis."

I looked over at the little white building that I had earlier thought was the gift shop. It made sense. That looked a lot more like a mission.

"It's not Mission Dolores. *That's* Mission Dolores." Mishie pointed at the really pretty gigantic church.

"But you said that wasn't the mission." Mark the know-it-all was trying to correct her. "That's the-"

"Just let me finish, okay?"

I snickered. "What's a 'Just let me finish, okay'?"

"So, Mission San Francisco got too small to hold all of the people that came to mass. Because of this, they had to build a new church. The new church they built was right next to Mission San Francisco. Since there couldn't be two churches standing next to each other, each having the same name, they only took part of the name, Mission, and called this big parish church 'Mission Dolores.' The Dolores part of the name came from 'Dolores Creek,' a small creek by the mission."

I looked around, hoping to see Dolores Creek. After a while, I stared at Mark. He was now supposed to say, "Oh, my goodness! There it is!" And I was supposed to say, "Where?" And he was supposed to say, "Right there! Don't you see it? There! Allison, you're blind!"

"Where is it, Mark?" I asked him. He was the one who usually found things before me.

"I don't see it," he said.

Mishie laughed. "That's because it doesn't exist anymore! Dolores Creek was filled up with dirt, and houses were built on top of it!"

"Why?" I asked. "We could have brought our swimming suits and gone swimming."

Mishie frowned. "First, that probably wouldn't have been allowed. Second, the water would be freezing cold. Third, I can't swim."

I sighed. I always have the worst ideas.

We went inside the gift shop, which was the entrance, and the lady at the counter told us we had to start our tour in the cemetery because there was a mass going on in the chapel. The tour usually starts in the chapel.

After Mishie said, "Mishie service," we went into the cemetery and started walking around. Mishie said that an Alfred Hitchcock movie, "Vertigo," was filmed in the cemetery of this mission. I found some of the gravestones really neat here, because they were like big cement poles. Except they weren't poles. They were thicker than poles, and had a pointy top. There was also a gigantic redwood tree in the center of the cemetery. It was huge! And I liked these super neat purple plants. One plant had large flower-like thingies, and the other one had small flower-like thingies.

There was also a statue of Father Junipero Serra that looked really good. I stood around it for a while admiring it. "Wow," I said. "Whoever did this was a really talented statue-maker."

"Statue-maker?" Mark laughed hysterically at me. "Isn't he called a sculptor? What kind of name is that? Statue-maker? Ha, ha, ha, ha!"

"Don't laugh at him, Mark. Especially if you think that statue's good. The 'statue-maker' was blind," said Mishie.

"Really?" I asked.

"Really," she replied. "His name was Arthur Putnam."

"Cool!"

Finally, I would like to mention this statue of a lamb that was in the dirt. The lamb was very cute. There was a bit of moss growing on her, though. I wondered what a lamb had to do with somebody's grave. After some more searching for the Golden Mission and touring, we decided to leave the cemetery.

Before going into the museum, there was this area that we stopped in that had a fountain in it. No fish, but there were quite a few coins in there.

Next, we went into the museum. I had just stepped in when a Father came in. His name was Father Ed, the mission priest, and he asked if I would like to meet the mission cat, Sally. You know what I said: yes…please. In a couple of minutes, Father Ed came back with Sally. She was soft and fluffy, and her fur was long and grayish. Her whiskers were long, too. She was in this papoose thingy, so she wouldn't be running away. Father Ed let me pet her, and she felt really nice and soft, just like Mr. Fwibble-Wibble.

Father Ed asked if we would like a special tour of the mission. He said he had some really cool stuff to show us. We said yes, because Mishie never showed us the *special* stuff, and we thought maybe if we learned new things, we could be closer to finding the Golden Mission.

Father Ed took us inside the chapel. We could tour the museum later.

As soon as we entered, the ceiling jumped out at me. It had an awesome design, and lots of beautiful colors.

"Those designs," said Mark, "are called chevrons. Indian chevrons."

"Like the gas station, Chevron?"

"No, like the things that look like the less than and greater than signs." (< and >).

"Oh, yeah. Those."

"Those are chevrons."

"I see…."

Mark also said that the chevrons were painted with bright vegetable dyes.

"It's only been painted over once," said Mishie. "In 1940 or so. Like they did before, they used vegetable dyes to paint the ceiling." Then she beamed, and showed off her really white teeth. I think she's been using the miniature version of those Crest Whitening Strips, because her teeth were abnormally white. I also think she was trying to show off in front of a real live Father.

Father Ed nodded, and told Mishie she was a smart fairy. I saw her blush. "And," Mishie added, hoping for another compliment, "the chapel's walls are 4 feet thick!" Father Ed didn't say anything that time, so Mishie tried again. "And, this was the first mission to be secularized!"

"Mishie," I said, "I don't think he wants to listen to you rambling on and on anymore. Anyway, what's secularized?"

"Oh," said Mishie, somewhat disappointed because Father Ed probably didn't want to listen to 30 hours of facts, "Anyway, being secularized is taking the missions away from the church and placing them in government rule."

"Thanks," I said.

Then, Father Ed told us to look at the altar. He named the statues that were standing in the six niches. The bottom left was Virgin Mary. You could tell because she was wearing the crown. The bottom center was a crucifix. It felt somewhat scary to me, because it was Jesus on the Cross, and he was all bloody. The bottom right was Santa Ana. The city of Santa Ana was named after her. On the top left was San Joaquin. There is also a city named after him. On the top center was San Miguel. He has a city named after him. Mishie says there's also a Mission named Mission San Miguel, but we won't be going there for a while. Santa Clara, the saint on the top right, also had a city and mission named after her. Mission Santa Clara is one we'll be going to tomorrow, right after Mission San Juan Capistrano.

"Would you like to ring the mission bells?" Father Ed asked. He is very nice. I said sure.

Since Mishie couldn't ring the bells, (she was too small) I thought I should ring two of the bells, and Mark should ring one. I deserved to ring two. I was working hard. Mark didn't deserve it.

"Okay, I ring two, you ring one," I said to Mark.

"Why do you get to ring two?" he asked.

"Because. I deserve it."

"You're saying I don't?"

"Yeah. Exactly."

"Why don't *I* deserve it? You need to learn to be fair."

"I'm being fair."

"No you're not."

"I am!"

"You're not."

"I *am!*"

"You're not."

"*I AM!*"

I can scream pretty loud. So I got to ring two bells. Mark obviously didn't want me screaming, because I saw him cover his ears when I screamed, "*I AM!*"

After we rang the bells, we started to tour the chapel, but Father Ed had more cool stuff to show us.

We went out into the cemetery. It was still raining, so Mark shared his umbrella with Father Ed, since Father Ed didn't have an umbrella. Father Ed showed us the grave of the first mayor, or Alcalde, of San Francisco – Don Francisco De Haro. Then he showed us the grave of Don Luis Antonio Arguello, the first governor of Alta California.

As we were walking to the tule reed home, I learned that the cemetery at Mission San Francisco is one of only two cemeteries in the entire city of San Francisco. The other one is The San Francisco National Cemetery/The Presidio.

San Francisco City and County is just forty-nine square miles. Land is really precious, so San Francisco's Board of Supervisors decided to move most of the cemeteries farther south. By around 1940, there were only two cemeteries left.

We then went inside the tule reed home. Father Ed said no matter how much it rained, no matter how big the storm was, it was always dry inside the tule reed home. He has never seen it wet inside.

Mishie said to us, "The Indians were buried in this cemetery, and then the Spaniards came, and when they died, they were buried on top of the Indians. So the tule reed home is a memorial to the Indians."

"Very good," Father Ed commented.

Mishie smiled and showed off her Crest Whitening Strip teeth. Then she giggled, which I have never heard her do before. It sounds very weird; it's like a little, high-pitched, "he, he!"

Father Ed left with adorable Sally, and we went back inside the chapel. I noticed the yellow stained-glass windows. They were neat. As I was walking around, I looked at the walls. They were white, and on one side there was a gigantic mural that didn't take up the whole wall. It was a painting of… well it looked like the inside of a church, because there was an altar, and there were lots of people inside it. Then I looked at a white baptismal that was surrounded by a fence.

As I finished my walk around the chapel, I started to stare constantly at the white, blank walls. The chapel seemed to be missing something.

"Mishie?" I asked. "What happened to the Stations of the Cross?"

"They're in the church," she said. This time she didn't smile or anything. She only did that around Father Ed. So yes, she was showing off.

Last, I looked at the grave of Lieutenant Don Jose Joaquin Moraga, one of the two leaders of this mission. There were two leaders for each mission. A church leader and an army leader. You would assume that the leader buried in the chapel was the church leader, but no. Don Jose Joaquin Moraga was the army leader!

Before going into the Basilica, we saw a diorama of the mission in a huge glass case. It was really neat, and it was a memorial to Frank J. Portman, who dedicated himself to the restoration of Mission San Francisco.

We did a little more walking, and then we went inside the big church, the one I had thought earlier was the real mission. We went in the side door, and as soon as I stepped inside, I saw a statue of Saint Martin de Porres. The reason I liked him a lot was because there were animals at his feet, and I love animals. There was a cat, dog, and mouse eating in peace from the same plate. He was also holding a broom, because he considered all work to be sacred no matter how menial.

Then, we started to tour the church. I noticed the stained glass windows as soon as I took my first peek inside. Instead of having pictures of Mary or Joseph or Jesus or someone like that, there were pictures of the other 20 California missions – because they left out Mission Dolores. Occasionally, there was a stained glass window with a priest on it. I saw one with Father Serra, and another with Father Palou. We looked at the stained glass windows, and Mishie showed us our next mission, Mission San Juan Capistrano.

After the three of us finished looking at the stained glass windows, we noticed the many palms stuck onto the sides on the pews. They were here because of Palm Sunday, which just recently passed. They looked like arches. They were super cool, and we went under them.

The Stations of the Cross were really neat. The people were gold, and the background was a bluish-green.

Last, our trio looked at the basilica conopaeum. This mission was a basilica. Unlike the basilica conopaeum at most of the basilica missions, this one was not hanging. It was just on a stand thingy. After that, we left the big church.

Since we didn't get to tour the museum thoroughly, we went back inside it. It only had one room. One of my favorite things in that room was the adobe bricks. They were being protected by a window-thingy. There were also fox pelts, acorns, abalone necklaces, arrowheads, chains, stakes, and vestments. I also saw a sign that said this museum was dedicated to Harry Downie, a man who had a lot to do with the history of the mission in Carmel (San Carlos).

We saw a model of the Chutchui Indians doing different tasks. One was in a kiicha (a hut) and one was playing. I really liked this model.

We walked out of the mission, and we were soon standing in front of it. It was time to leave.

"We're leaving now, right?" asked Mark. I wasn't the only one getting used to the system.

"Yeah," said Mishie, and soon I could no longer see old Mission San Francisco (a.k.a. Mission Dolores).

"So…" I started to start a conversation. "Where are we staying?"

"The first non-expensive hotel I see with a vacancy sign."

"Okay…" That could take a while. I mean, finding a *non-expensive* hotel in San Francisco.

Apparently, Mishie is very good at finding stuff. We found a motel, that was sort of small, but the room was cozy, and had two beds. I liked this a lot because I hate sleeping with Mark. He kicks me in his sleep (he always dreams he is a wrestling guy, something he is obsessed with), drools on my hair (this turns out really gross in the morning), and I tend to have really bad dreams when we sleep in the same bed (I always dream I am wrestling against him…and I lose. Now, that's a nightmare!).

    I fell asleep comfortably, and without Mark (Hooray!).

Favorite Things at Mission San Francisco

1. When we were in the museum, Father Ed brought in **Sally**, the amazingly adorable **mission cat**. She was soooooo cute! I loved petting her, and having a special tour with Father Ed was really cool. Thank you, Father Ed, for showing me Sally and giving us that special detailed tour!

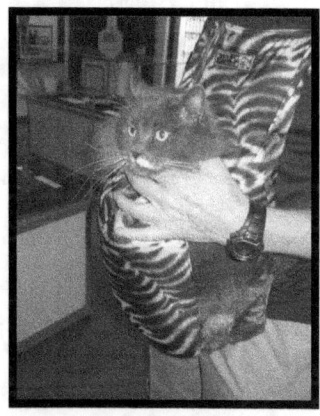

2. I found the **ceiling** in the **church** really different! There were all sorts of colorful zigzag designs on it, and Mark said it was painted with vegetable dyes. I thought this was neat, too.
3. Near the side door of the Basilica, was a **statue** of **Saint Martin de Porres**. It had a **dog, cat**, and **mouse** eating in peace from the same plate at his feet. I enjoyed him a lot!
4. When we were taking our special tour of the mission with Father Ed, he let us **ring the bells**. It was very fun, and I loved the sound.
5. Inside the Basilica, there were **stained glass windows** that had pictures of the other **20 California missions** on them. I really enjoyed looking at these.
6. In the **cemetery**, the **first governor of Alta California** and the **first mayor of San Francisco** were **buried**. Also, there was a very good **statue of Father Junipero Serra** created by a blind sculptor, Arthur Putnam. It amazed me how someone who was blind could make a sculpture so good. And, by somebody's grave there was a little **statue of a white lamb**. There was a bit of moss growing on her, but I still found the statue cute. I wondered what a lamb had to do with somebody's grave. Maybe the person buried there was a lamb fanatic or something!

Mission Seven

Mission San Juan Capistrano
(Founded: 1776)

San Juan Capistrano, CA

Jewel of the Missions

Seventh Mission: Mission San Juan Capistrano

*W*e hovered above the ground a few inches before Mishie said, "Land," and we hit the concrete.

Mark, Mishie, and I were right in front of our next mission, Mission San Juan Capistrano. It's the Jewel of the Missions. I saw an entrance, and said, "That way."

We went in, and we found that we were in a room where you buy tickets. When we were at the counter, Mishie said, "Mishie service," before the lady could say anything, and the door swung forward.

The first thing we saw was a table with a bunch of things that looked like remote controls on it. A man was there. He gave one to Mark, one to me, and he didn't see Mishie, so he didn't give one to her. Mishie didn't need one anyway.

It turns out these are audio things that give you information about each stop at Mission San Juan Capistrano. Mark and I just put them in our pockets because we had Mishie to tell us about everything.

The first stop was a plaque that told us all about the mission. Mark, the weirdo, wanted to read the sign because he thought it would help us find clues. I wanted to get a move on, and actually search the mission, not piddle around at signs. *That* would actually help us find clues. Somehow, Mishie made us compromise, and she summarized up the sign. I don't know how she does it.

Next, we looked at the Olive Mill, a device used for mashing olives to make products. This was used to make olive oil, olive juice, and other items using olives.

Then, the three of us went into the soldiers' barracks. There were two beds on either side, a table for four in the center, and two very large pictures on the wall. In the front of the room, there was a glass case holding uniforms worn and weapons used.

When we had exited, finding no clues, we all entered the kiicha. It is a replica of a hut the Acjachemen (Uh–hah –

chee–men) tribe might have built. Inside, there was a circle of rocks that was used to build a fire. When I looked up, there was a hole in the top. When I asked Mishie what this was for, she said it let the smoke out from the fires the Indians made in the kiicha. Outside, there was a giant stone with holes in it. The Indians used the stone and some other rocks to grind acorns. Mark picked up an acorn.

"Evidence," he said.

"Yeah," I said. Not like I meant it. A piece of parchment with mysterious writing on it is evidence.

Afterwards, Mark, Mishie and I went inside the Padre's Kitchen. There were really cool items in there that I liked. For instance, the broom, the pot, the humongous pot, the gourd, the stove, and the potato were all really neat. The only thing I didn't like in there was the carrot. (Yuck! I hate carrots, which is probably why Mark loves them.)

The next place we visited was the mission pantry. Food was stacked on the shelves. There were also pots in the pantry. A ladder led up to the second floor.

Subsequently, we went into a place Father Jose Moot used for a house. The room where you entered had a one–person table, a bench and a fireplace. The next room was the guest room where Father Moot let guests sleep. He climbed up a ladder to the second floor where he slept. He pulled up the ladder so bandits and thieves couldn't reach him.

For a while, we explored more of Father Moot's house. We saw the dining room, and lots more. Finally we came into a room describing the Acjachemen Indians.

In there, we saw a coyote skin, some tools, spearheads arrowheads, and an abalone shell.

The next room contained a wine vat. The very first wine vat in California was here, at Mission San Juan Capistrano. How do I know? Mark told me. He actually read the sign. (Like he always does; like I always don't.)

We went outside and looked at another wine vat. Then, we saw a cow's skin hung on the brick wall. The cow skin had the brand of Mission San Juan Capistrano on it. It felt soft, so I liked it. Mark said it was, "Yuck! Gross, Allison! You actually touch that stuff? Eeeewww!" Then he made an odd shivering movement, which was supposed to emphasize the fact that he was grossed out. But Mark is not a very good actor, so when he did this, it looked dumb.

After passing the remains of an old adobe brick wall, we looked at the Catalan Furnaces. I think they were used for making soap. None of us are completely sure.

We all walked through the garden, under a grapevine, and along a brick bridge. The brick bridge was not exactly a bridge. It was like a walkway that let you see more tallow vats. It was like a bridge because there were vats on either side.

We all walked further and we passed the Tallow Cooking Stove. Tallow, a valuable product made of animal fat, was used in candles, grease, ointment, and soap production.

Next, we visited an outside church. Or was it a picnic area? There was a statue of a person in the back, and there were wooden seats to sit on in front of it. That's probably why I thought it was a church. We passed the Tallow Cooking Stove again, and started making our way to a room with a weaving loom and displays of products made. There was a window with wavy glass that I liked. In the next room, there was a piano with a sheet of music on the top. Then, we went into a room with lots of interesting pictures on the walls.

After exiting, we went into a room about Leon Rene, a man who composed a song called, "When the Swallows Come Back to Capistrano." Mishie said that one day, Leon Rene was waiting for his wife to serve breakfast while watching the news. The newscaster said that the swallows were sighted coming back to Mission San Juan Capistrano. He said to his wife, "Must I wait until the swallows come back to Capistrano to get my breakfast?" That one sentence gave him the idea of the song he later composed. There was a piano in the room, a desk, and an electric fan. I don't understand why the electric fan was in there.

We walked through the garden, and awed at what looked like a giant asparagus. (Ick! It still looked cool, though.) There were also little things on a tree that were red, sometimes yellow, and had soft spikes. When I crushed one, Mark covered his eyes and orange stuff came out.

Not too soon afterward, Mark, Mishie and I strolled to a Koi fountain. There were beautiful fish swimming around the fountain. One yellow one led a huge group of fish around in a circle. I could have watched them for hours. Mark could have said, "Hurry up, Ally, we don't have all day!" for hours. After a super long time, we left the Koi pond.

After walking through a bit more, we came into the Serra Chapel, the last remaining church where Father Serra held services. Inside, almost everything looked golden. There were gold statues up front, and they stood on gold shelves. But no Golden Mission.

There was also a very old baptismal on display. If you don't know what that is, it's okay, I didn't know either until Mr. Intelligent told me. A baptismal is a thing that looks like a bathtub that babies get baptized in. The priest says something like, "In the name of the Father, Son, and the Holy Spirit! I now give you your name, Mark Weirdo Noodlehead!" This is not Mark's real name, but I wish it were. Then, the priest bathes the baby in holy water.

We exited the chapel into a cemetery. The most eye-catching grave was the one of Monsignor St. John O' Sullivan. He was the pastor at the old mission for 23 out of his 59 years.

I decided to look around. There was a brown gate. It was closed. I thought I would look in through the bars. I walked there, with Mark and Mishie following me, wondering where I was going. Mark was going to say something, but Mishie stopped him, thinking we were going to get into another argument.

When we looked through the gate, I saw that there were bunches of pink flowers everywhere, a fountain in the middle of the flowers, and there was a small statue of Father Junipero Serra very far off to the right. We watched the crows fly back and away, back and away until Mishie said, "We're running late. I think you guys might want to consider leaving."

"Okay," said Mark.

We soon were outside, in an area where bells were rung. We dipped our hands into the fountain, listened to the audio thing, (it was much faster than Mishie, who couldn't stop talking) and headed out, ready to visit our next stop, the Great Stone Church.

The Great Stone Church was the remains of the church that used to stand at Mission San Juan Capistrano. It used to be the largest of all the mission churches in Alta California, but it was destroyed in an earthquake. You could still see the little shelves that the statues used to stand on. Walking back, we saw two original bells that used to be on the bell tower. Then, we decided to go and revisit the Koi fish.

Our last stop was the wishing well. When Mark and I looked at all the coins inside, we were amazed.

"That's a lot of money!" I said.

"Yeah," Mark agreed with me for the first time in his life. Well, maybe. It could have been the second...

"Why don't you guys make wishes?" Mishie suggested.

"Okay," we said together.

"I wish that Allison falls off the edge of the earth into deep space where there is no oxygen, only carbon dioxide, and she can't breathe, so she dies, and I build a Styrofoam dummy of her that does whatever I want it to at home in replace of her," wished Mark.

"I heard that!" I yelled at him.

"So?"

"So you told me your wish and now it's not going to come true!"

"I didn't tell it to you, you eavesdropped."

"Did not!"

"I disagree."

"Whatever."

"Yes, whatever. You make your wish now."

"Okay. I wish that Mark falls off a cliff into a dark lagoon with no bottom, and he can't see anything, but it turns out this lagoon is the place where the Loch Ness Monster lives and the Loch Ness Monster comes and eats him for breakfast, and I throw all his toys and his computer in the lagoon and the

Loch Ness Monster eats those for lunch because they taste good like Mark." I thought my wish was better than Mark's.

We exited Mission San Juan Capistrano, and visited the church behind it–Mission Basilica San Juan Capistrano. This church was built in an attempt to replicate the Great Stone Church that was destroyed by an earthquake in 1812. The new church was completed and dedicated in 1987. It is 15% larger than the Great Stone Church so it can hold 800 worshippers at a time.

The Basilica is on mission property, just like the school, but it isn't really part of the actual mission grounds. Remember to exit the mission, and then go see it.

When we got there, the first thing I saw was the baptismal. It was made out of marble. We walked down farther, and just stared at the architecture. There were statues standing on shelves that looked real. I spotted the basilica conopaeum. It's the fourth and final one we will see.

When Mishie said we had to go, we finally left. We entered the mission for the last time. I took some final pictures of the Koi pond, and we really left.

When we were standing outside the mission, Mishie said, "Time to leave." And we were soon soaring above the clouds.

Favorite Things at Mission San Juan Capistrano

1. Inside the mission, there are two fountains, both containing **Koi fish**. Watch the Koi swim for a while, it's really cool.
2. There is a **grape vine** at the mission. If you're daring enough, try a grape (but don't get caught, because you're not allowed to do this). They are delicious, and will not kill you. I have eaten one.
3. When I visited the mission, there was a **bird, snacking** on a cactus **prickly pear**. If you see a bird eating prickly pear, make sure you keep watching.
4. After leaving the room about Leon Rene, we saw a tree that had little **squishy berry–like thingies**. When you squashed them, orange goo came out.
5. After touring the garden, we went into the **kiicha,** a cool Indian hut that the Indians lived in. It was fun to pretend we were Indians inside it, and look through the hole in the top.
6. On our way to the Great Stone Church, Mishie told us that a **ghost** was supposed to appear out of a certain **window** in the building. The window she pointed out had little black lines all over it, like spider webs. I could easily imagine a ghost appearing there.
7. Inside the chapel there was a **huge crack in the wall**. I'm pretty sure they put it there on purpose, but you never know!
8. As soon as you enter the mission, there is a garden. Inside this garden, there are many plants, including the **Bird of Paradise plant**. It is soooooo pretty. You need to see it.

Mission Eight

Mission Santa Clara de Asis
(Founded: 1777)

Santa Clara, CA

No Known Nickname

Eighth Mission: Mission Santa Clara

*T*his was taking a looooong time. Well, Mission San Juan Capistrano was way down south, and Mission Santa Clara was way up north. I sighed. This was boring. We were now flying over a college campus. I read the sign. It said, "Santa Clara University." Well, at least we were in Santa Clara. I wondered how far it was to the mission.

I suddenly felt myself being pulled downward by some weird force. "Whoa! Mishie, we're not there yet!"

"Yes, we are," she replied.

"No. We're not. A mission isn't going to be just standing here in the middle of a college campus."

"Then what's that?" Mishie was pointing to…Mission Santa Clara.

"What?" This couldn't be right. "Are you an illusionist or something like that, Mishie?"

"No," she laughed. "Mission Santa Clara is located on a college campus. It's no illusion. In fact, it's the oldest college of higher learning in California."

We landed in front of Mission Santa Clara and I looked around. It was small, but it was really pretty. The church had these neat decorations on it.

"This was the first mission that was named after a woman saint. Saint Clare was its patroness saint," said Mishie.

If you don't have Mishie to give you a tour, I recommend starting at the information desk. It is to the left of the mission in the Benson Center, building #301. If they are closed, then walk into the mission church and to the right is a visitor's center with self guided maps. You can also find a great self guided tour on the web at www.scu.edu/missionchurch/history/upload/Self_Guided_Tour-3.pdf. In the Benson Center, you will also find the gift shop located inside the campus bookstore.

We started our tour of the mission. Outside it, there was a giant cross that had these words on it: "He that shall persevere to the end, he shall be saved." It's a quote from the bible. And at the bottom it said, Matthew XXIV. 13.

In front of the church, there were small white crosses stuck into the ground. Mishie said they were placed there in 1989 by Santa Clara University students as a memorial to eight murdered El Salvadorians.

Mark, Mishie and I went into the courtyard. To enter, we had to walk under this really pretty wisteria vine. According to Mishie (and the brochure), it was over 130 years old. It had small purple flowers growing on it, and I put one in my hair. You weren't allowed to pull the flowers off, so I just picked one up off the ground. The little purple flowers only bloom around Easter time, so we had good timing and good luck.

The trunk was really large and twisted, and I made Mark take a picture of me by it after a small argument.

Then, we saw a statue of Jesus Christ. He had flowers around the base of his pedestal, and they were really cool. I think they are called monkey face flowers, but I'm not completely sure. They were yellow or purple around the edges, but in the middle they were black or brown.

We strolled around the courtyard some more, and did a little searching for the Golden Mission. I noticed that a door was open. I read the sign, and it said this was the chapel.

Usually, the chapel wasn't open to the public. And today was no different. They were just getting ready for a special event, and the door happened to be open. Uninvited, we walked in. The lady in the chapel could have said, "Get out, you people! What do you think you are doing? This isn't open to the public! Get out!" But she didn't say that. She let us tour the chapel.

Inside, there were twenty chairs. Each had a picture of one of the California missions carved in it. There were only 20 because one was missing. I couldn't figure out which one it was (I haven't been to all of the missions). However, I think I saw two or three of Mission Santa Clara, so I couldn't really figure these chairs out. After a little more exploring in the chapel, we wanted to go to lunch. So that's what we did.

I voted for Subway, and Mark voted for Quizno's. Since Mishie was fine with whatever we got, she suggested that we do rock-paper-scissors. This wasn't that good of an idea because...Mark won. Well, Quizno's isn't *that* bad.

After lunch, we decided to tour the church. We came in the side door of the church and I saw a life-size statue of Jesus on the Cross. Mishie said it was called the Catala Crucifix. It was carved in Mexico, and then it was brought to the mission in 1802. It was saved from the 1926 fire.

"There was a father at the mission, Father Catala, who loved this statue. He loved it so much, that when he died, he was buried at the foot of it."

I know Father Catala loved the crucifix, but it was so detailed, it scared me. I covered my face with the notepad Mark and I share so I wouldn't have to look at it. When Mark stepped inside, he saw it, and reached for the notepad he used to have in his pocket. But I had stolen it from him. He looked at the crucifix again and shivered. For, like, two seconds, I actually felt *sorry* for him, but then I remembered he was my weird, annoying, know-it-all brother, and I quit feeling sorry.

So nobody would think Mark was a scardey-cat, he looked at it one more time without winching. Then he looked away for the rest of the time we were in the church. So I was the only one actually searching for the Golden Mission. He was trying his best to not look at the Catala Crucifix, but sometimes, it was unavoidable.

Aside from the Catala Crucifix, I liked the church quite a bit. The Stations of the Cross were beautiful, and I really liked the silvery-colored organ in the balcony.

"This church is wider than most mission churches," said Mishie.

"Why?" I asked.

"Well," she replied, "The 5th Santa Clara church burned down in the 1926 fire. They didn't rebuild it using adobe, but something else that was sturdier, and since this material was better, the church didn't have to be so narrow. It could be widened. So they built a wider mission church, and there were no pews. Instead, they used chairs. Because of this, they can arrange the chairs however they want, for any event they're having."

I raised my eyebrows. Mishie was so detailed with everything. "My question has been answered."

There were a lot of confessionals here. But they didn't look like confessionals, really. They looked like…red curtains. I looked behind all of the red curtains, which was pretty fun.

The ceiling was also really neat. There were lots of big diamonds painted on it. The diamonds were red, and the background was green.

We walked a little further, and then we saw a baptismal well. It was just set up for Easter, but it was very pretty. There were flowers by the cross that was standing behind the well.

After that, Mark, Mishie, and I looked at the altar. There were three statues in three niches. Then, I looked down from the altar, and I saw these…heads. Not real human heads, but statues of heads. If they had bodies, (which I highly doubt) then they were covered up by a table. The ceiling above the altar was really pretty. There were these little angel people flying around in the clouds.

"The altar is pretty," I said to Mishie. "Do you know who made it?"

"Not really. But it was reproduced under the direction of Harry Downie," she said.

I also liked a humongous notebook that people would write prayers and thank yous to God in. I read one and it said stuff like: "Dear Lord, thank you for my wonderful family. Please bless them with good health, and cure [insert their name] from his/her cold. Thank you for all the blessing you give me. Amen." I thought it was cool. They didn't have this at any of the other missions.

We exited out of the side door of the church. When we got out, we saw this statue of St. Augustine of Hippo. This made me laugh because my dad likes to get "hippo," which means, "touch" in another language. He likes to be touched.

After that, we went to see the rose garden. We walked all the way there just to see that the gate was locked. We still got to peek inside, though.

"This used to be the cemetery," said Mishie. "That's why it says rose garden/cemetery on your tour maps."

The three of us went to see a statue of Father Junipero Serra, which didn't take too long, and then we went to see the old adobe wall that had survived the 1926 fire. It was just a fragment of a wall that used to surround the mission, protecting it from the outside world. But it didn't do that now. It just opened up to the college campus.

After that, we went back under the wisteria vine, and looked at a map of the mission. It had some really neat facts on it. Mark made me write them down so, "the readers could have some real information instead of this stupid then we went here, and then we went there stuff." Whatever, you noodlehead!

One of the mission bells was a gift from Carlos III of Spain. Father Catala, a recognized mission Father, is buried in the church. The adobe wall survived the 1926 earthquake. The rose garden used to be a cemetery. You already know the last three.

"Technically, we're done with our tour," said Mishie.

"Technically? How are we *technically* done with the tour?" asked Mark.

"What does technically mean?"

Mark looked at me with the wow-you-seriously-don't-know-what-that-means look and I looked at him with the yeah-do-you-have-a-problem-with-that look. He said yes with his eyes.

"Well," said Mishie. "It's hard to explain. It means, like, um…yes and no at the same time…kind of. I guess…uh…you'll figure it out later."

Mark, who is very good at explaining, jumped in. "Like Mishie said, technically means yes and no at the same time. You can persuade somebody that the answer is yes, and you can also persuade them that the answer is no. But really, the answer is sort of."

"Yeah, I kind of get what you mean," I said.

I soon figured out what technically meant. Mishie flew us to a grassy area, where we landed.

"Due to various problems, the mission was moved to many different locations," said Mishie.

"Problems?" I asked. "What kind of problems?"

"Water problems, flood problems, earthquake problems, food problems..."

"Okay. I get it."

"First, it was located by the Guadalupe River. But it got flooded out, so they moved it. There were problems there so they moved it here, to its third location. This location lasted for a long time, but eventually, it was moved. In the end, the mission was moved to 5 different locations. And 6 Mission Santa Clara's were built. The one we were just at was the 6th *mission* on the 5th *location*.

"Where we are now is where the third mission was built. I thought I'd bring you here because... you know, the Golden Mission could be here."

Mark read the plaques, and when he was done with that, he joined me in searching for the Golden Mission. Unfortunately, we didn't find any clues or anything similar to a clue. But I did see some markings in the street. It was stamped concrete. When I asked Mishie what they were for, she said that's an outline of where the rooms used to be at Mission Santa Clara.

"Now," said Mishie. "Our tour is not *technically* done; it's done!"

I laughed. I laugh easily. I have learned that Mark doesn't. When I looked at him, he was looking at me like he was going to say, "Why in the world are you laughing? That wasn't even close to funny!" I gave him the it's-not-my-fault-you-don't-understand-me look. I give him this look too often, but, well, he just doesn't understand me. It's the truth!

After an extremely long time, Mishie said, "Okay...are we going to leave this mission, or are we too busy giving each other dirty looks?"

"Um...uh...no. We're gonna leave." Then I nodded at Mark, who just shook his head at me. Then he gave me a look I didn't recognize. I have a feeling that look was probably the Allison-you-are-just-so-stupid look.

"You said we were going to leave. Aren't we?" Mishie seemed to be getting impatient.

Before I could answer, Mishie heaved us up in the air.

Favorite Things at Mission Santa Clara

1. To enter the courtyard, we had to go under a really neat **wisteria arbor**. The flowers growing on it were very pretty, and they were my favorite color, purple. They only blossom around Easter, but the vines will probably still be beautiful without flowers. Also, the trunk was really twisted.
2. When we were coming out of the side door of the church, I noticed a **statue** of **St. Augustine of Hippo**. I got a kick out of this because my father likes to get "hippo," which means "touch" in a different language.
3. As we were leaving, I saw a **chipmunk or squirrel** or some animal like that run across the grass. He was really cute!
4. In the **chapel**, there were **chairs** each with a carving of a mission on them. There were only 20, though, because one was missing. This confused me, because I saw maybe 2 or 3 chairs that had Mission Santa Clara on them.
5. On the altar in the church, there were these **statues of…heads**. If they had bodies, a table was hiding them. I don't think they did, though. I liked looking at the heads, even though they were sort of weird.
6. Near the St. Augustine of Hippo statue, there were very pretty **Bird of Paradise plants**. If you take a close-up picture of them, they look really cool.
7. Some **stone steps** were on display in front of the El Camino Real bell. They were used to get passengers in and out of carriages. They said "S. C. C.," on them, which stood for Santa Clara College.

Mission Nine

Mission San Buenaventura
(Founded: 1782)

Ventura, CA

* *Mission by the Sea*

Ninth Mission: Mission San Buenaventura

I closed my eyes and felt the wind in my face. When I opened them, Mishie was pointing downward and saying, "There it is!"

Mark and I looked down. There was Mission San Buenaventura, Mission by the Sea. If I stretched my neck, and looked through the clouds, I *could* see the ocean.

The mission was located where you would least expect a mission to be. Around it were restaurants and more. Directly across from it, there was a fountain that I thought was *really* cool. It had a regular fountain on one end, but then, the water flowed out and it was like a creek. The creek ended, and then there was another fountain. I thought it was like a giant fountain barbell. I followed it all the way down.

Next to the mission were two large trees. It wasn't even close to Christmas, but there were lights on them. I asked Mishie why they were there, and she said that the lights stayed up all the time, every day. But they were turned on only around Christmas time. They are on from the first Saturday in December to around New Year's Day.

When the three of us landed outside the gift shop, which was the entrance to the mission, we all went inside.

"Mishie service," said Mishie, without looking at the person at the front desk.

Then, we climbed up the stairs leading to the museum.

The museum was my favorite place at the mission. That's why almost all of my favorite things were in the museum. There was a pair of wooden shoes, an old wooden mission bell, and a ukulele thing; all of which I enjoyed. Some other things I admired included a confessional in the back, a model of the mission, the original front doors in the back, and some Indian tools.

When we stepped outside, Mark, Mishie and I were in a courtyard. Fine-looking plants were scattered throughout the garden.

The next place we went was the church. In a room to the left, which was gated off, there were some band instruments.

"This room," said Mishie, "is actually a baptistery. It's just different now."

Farther down, we all stopped to look at the altar. It reminded me of one of those Roman coliseums. When I shared this with Mark, he said I was crazy.

I said he was crazier.

He said I was the craziest.

I said he was still crazier than me.

He said he was not.

I said he was.

He apparently didn't want to get into "Is not!" "Is too!" fight, so he called me a different name.

He said I was a typical sister.

I said he was a noodlehead, because I didn't know what a typical sister was. When he says something I don't understand, I just use this great backup, "You're a noodlehead." I use it too much, but it is helpful.

He asked me what kind of name that was.

I said it was a name describing him.

I didn't notice it, but instead of whispering inside the church, we had begun yelling. That is why Mishie had to usher us out of the church.

"You're both crazy!" Mishie exclaimed suddenly, when we were walking to our next destination. "Arguing with each other instead of trying to find the Golden Mission! What kind of search is this?"

"An argue–search?" I suggested, hoping to make a joke. They both acted like it wasn't funny, even though it was hilarious. (It was, right? I'm hilarious!)

Now, Mishie was acting like she never said that thing about the Golden Mission, and things were back to normal. Except for Mark.

Mark wasn't talking to me because of the little thing that happened in the church, and instead he was drawing on his notepad. He told me he was taking notes, but when I looked over at him, I saw a dreadful picture of a knight fighting a fire-breathing dragon.

Mishie looked over at the notepad and frowned. So Mark would actually be writing something, she said, "Did you know that this was the last mission Father Serra founded?"

"Yes," I said.

"Yes," Mark said.

"And it was founded on Easter Sunday," Mishie added.

"Mm–hmm," That was nice to know.

"Oh, cool!" said Mark, and turned to a blank page on his notepad. Then he started writing stuff down.

Mishie saw that Mark was interested in facts now so she decided to talk more. "And, this mission's church has walls that are 6 ½ feet thick. The wooden chandeliers in the church were made by Harry Downie, and this was planned to be the third mission, but it actually ended up being the ninth for some reason."

By now, Mark was writing furiously on our notepad, loading the pages with unneeded facts. I was really mad at Mishie because she made Mark waste 8 perfectly good pages of our notepad.

After a little bit of walking, we found ourselves at a tomb. There were three Padres from the church buried there. Also, there was a settling tank near the tomb. Plus, there was a statue that had figures of turtles near the base. I wondered if turtles had anything to do with the mission. (That'd be cool if they did! Imagine the nickname: Mission of the Turtles!)

The back part of the mission was destroyed in order to build Holy Cross School. It is a beautiful school, in my opinion. Yet, I am sad that that part of the mission is gone. The Golden Mission could have been somewhere in there. (But, I doubt it, because the construction people would have told everybody if they found something.)

When we left the tomb, we started working our way to the exit of the mission. We stopped at an olive press. Mark, Mishie and I all liked it.

Soon, we had reached the exit. Our tour was over. In a few minutes' time, we had taken off into the air.

"Land," said Mishie. "I see where we're staying."

I landed, and Mark did, too. We went inside the hotel, and Mishie pulled a regular sized credit card out of her teeny, tiny, pocket.

I gasped. "Whoa! How did you do that?" It was like when Mary Poppins pulled that giant umbrella or whatever out of her purse.

"Magic," Mishie replied.

Mishie swiped the credit card in the credit card thing, and we took the elevator up to our room. I fell asleep very quickly.

Favorite Things at Mission San Buenaventura

1. In the museum, there was a **wooden bell** that I really liked. According to the sign, this mission was the only one that had wooden bells. But Mishie disagrees, and I agree with her disagreement. (I know it sounds funny.)
2. There was a very **long fountain** across the street from this mission. I followed it all the way down.
3. In the front of Holy Cross School, there was a statue of a lady. Right by her feet were a bunch of **turtles**! They were all looking at her feet as if they were super special or something. I thought it was funny and cool.
4. Mishie let us **light some candles** inside the church. I got a blue one, and Mark did, too. Lighting the candles was great!
5. Also, there were some **wooden molds** for making **shoes** in the museum. I thought those were neat.
6. I liked a **ukulele** or guitar or something that was in the museum. It was fantastic. (It was probably a ukulele because it had four strings.)
7. There was a **model** of **Mission San Buenaventura** *in the museum.* It was hard to believe that the mission was once as large as they made it look in the model.
8. I liked a **confessional** that was in the museum. It looked really neat.

Mission Ten

Mission Santa Barbara
(Founded: 1782)

Santa Barbara, CA

*Queen of the Missions

Tenth Mission: Mission Santa Barbara

Mark, Mishie, and I arrived in front of Mission Santa Barbara, the Queen of the Missions.

Before going inside, we looked at the lavanderia, the place where Indian ladies washed their clothes and took baths. We also checked out the fountain. At first, there were a bunch of pigeons sitting on the fountain. When we walked up, they all flew away. Mark said it was my weirdness that made them fly away. But, I knew it was his weirdness that made them fly away.

In a few minutes, all three of us were inside the gift shop, the starting point of the tour.

"Mishie service?" asked the clerk. She must be familiar with fairy tour guide thingies.

"Yes," said Mishie.

Inside the first room of the museums, there were things the Indians used such as arrowheads, spearheads, and baskets. There was also a tool used for grinding acorns on display, but I don't know what it is called.

The next room was the priest's bedroom. They had his bed in a glass display along with a chair, a desk, and a few paintings. In a glass display on the opposite side, there was a telescope. It was the biggest telescope I had seen in my whole life! It is probably, like, 3 feet long!

Next, we went into a room with lots of statues. There were three on each side, and they were chained off so no one could touch them. My favorite thing about this room was that you got to make a crayon rubbing of the mission. (Look at <u>Favorite Things</u> for more details about the crayon rubbing.)

The next room showed all of the different jobs at the mission. The case with blacksmithing items had hammers, nails, horseshoes, and other metal items on display. There was also a carpenter's display, a pottery display, a weaving display, a candle–making display, and a noodlehead display. The display about noodleheads said that there was only one noodlehead in the world and his name was Mark. He lives in Noodle, Weirdoland, and his favorite hobby was putting noodles on his head while reading signs. (In case you didn't figure it our already, I'm kidding about the noodlehead display.)

The next room was the bishop's room.

"Out of all the missions," said Mishie in the I'm-going-to-give-you-a-fact-now-listen-closely voice, "The first bishop of California stayed here, at Mission Santa Barbara." Wow!

After that, the three of us visited the kitchen. There was a lot of food on the table, and there were two stoves in the back for cooking.

Then, we went into the room with Island of the Blue Dolphins on display. It was a book about the Lost Woman of Saint Nicholas Island, who was brought to the mission after 18 years, of being stranded on the island. She and her brother missed a ship that left the island with the other Indians. Her brother was attacked by wild dogs, and she was the only one left. You would think that the other members of the tribe had reached the mainland safely, but no. The ship sank. So, Karana (that's her name) was the last Indian surviving of that tribe. She was buried at the mission in 1853.

Soon, Mark, Mishie and I were strolling around in the courtyard. In the middle of the courtyard, there was a beautiful fountain, surrounded by tall palm trees. We walked all around the border of the courtyard, since it was gated off.

After smelling the roses, and just walking around a bit more, Mark, Mishie and I went into the cemetery. First, we went into this building with what looked like just plaques on the walls. We all stepped inside.

"What are those?" Mark questioned.

"I think I know," I said. "Those are *plaques*. Right, Mark?" I said this in a voice that always annoyed him, a voice that would make him feel humiliated.

"Actually," said Mishie. "They aren't plaques. These are like doors." She tapped on one. "You open it up, and slide somebody's casket inside."

"Casket?" I inquired.

"Coffin." Mishie said.

On the way out, Mark grinned at me unpleasantly. I stuck my tongue out at him. It's so upsetting when I'm wrong.

We started our walk around the cemetery. All it really is is a bunch of gravestones and burials. Mishie said that there were approximately 4,000 Indians buried in the cemetery, and the last Indian buried in the cemetery was Tomas Ignacio Aquino in 1952. After searching some for the Golden Mission, we finally entered the church.

Above the doorway, there were three skull and crossbones carved in the stone. On the map/guide, it said that skulls and crossbones were carved over the entrance to the *cemetery*. The thing I don't get was that the figures were carved into the entrance of the *church*. I didn't really figure that out. Maybe they figure you enter the cemetery from the church.

When we were inside the church, Mark, Mishie and I all started looking around. In the back, there was a baptismal, along with another room. In that room, there was a statue in a niche and a really pretty thingy under the statue. I cannot explain the thingy under the statue; you will have to see it for yourself. Then, you'll see what I mean. Mishie thought it was a sanctuary, which is where they keep the communion host and the wine for masses (church services).

Some things that were interesting in the church included some giant paintings on the wall. Mishie said that they were the largest paintings that were ever put up in any mission's church. Another fascinating thing was that some Reverends, Brothers, and Fathers were buried under the church. There was a stone on the ground that listed all of the names of the Reverends, Brothers, and Fathers. Mishie said that every two years, some people went down and made sure that they were all okay. After a long while, the three of us had exited the church.

Before leaving, we searched the grounds for the Golden Mission a little more. I thought the trees and plants in the botanic garden were really nice.

In a few minutes, Mark, Mishie and I were standing outside the exit.

"1, 2, 3!" said Mishie, and we were flying away once again.

Favorite Things at Mission Santa Barbara

1. In one room, they were displaying **Island of the Blue Dolphins**, by Scott O'Dell. It is a book about the Lost Woman of Saint Nicholas Island, who was stranded on the island for 18 years. In real life, she was brought to the mission after she was rescued.
2. On the **front** of the mission, there was a **circular window** that looked really neat. Make sure you see it.
3. By the **courtyard**, there was a set of stairs. I looked at the stairs, and they led straight into a wall. I called them the **Stairs to Nowhere**! (Even though a wall isn't considered nowhere…)
4. In the **cemetery**, there was a **gigantic fig tree** from Australia with gigantic roots. It was super tall, and super spectacular!
5. When we were exiting the cemetery, and entering the church, we saw three **skull and crossbones** above the entrance to the church. They looked really neat, but I just can't figure out why they were over the entrance to the *church.*
6. In another room, there was a tile that had a raised picture of Mission Santa Barbara on it. It was on a table along with crayons and paper. You got to make a **crayon rubbing of the mission**.
7. When it rained, the water would come down on the roof, and land on the ground. But, when I looked down from the sloped roof, there was a **long cement ditch** thingamabob that had a drain at the end. So, instead of over watering the plants, the water would just be drained and saved for future use. Smart!

Mission Eleven

Mission La Purisima Concepcion
(Founded: 1787)

Lompoc, CA
The Linear Mission

Eleventh Mission: Mission La Purisima

"*I*s that it?" I asked. "It's so *different!*"

"That's it," Mishie informed. "It's just a different color. And instead of having it built in a quadrangle, like most missions, it's in a straight line. That's why it's called the linear mission."

I asked if this was the mission because . . . well . . . it looked different. Like Mishie said, it was a different color. Like a salmony color.

Soon, we were landing. The first things that caught my eye were animal pens outside the mission. There were a bunch of different creatures inside. It was like a farm. I could see horses, cows, and a huge ox with huge horns to match. It was in a pen by itself. I wonder why?

If I stretched my neck, I could see more pens. Pigs, chickens, and turkeys were in those. One turkey, a white one, was all puffed up and strutting around the pen like it owned the world. The other regular black turkeys were staring at it.

It was a rather long walk down to the mission. On the way there, we saw some cow hides hanging on a rack. Mark read the sign, (I never do) and he said that the cleaned and dried cowhides were traded with Yankee sailors in exchange for other things the mission needed.

Next, we went into an Indian cemetery. Many Indians were buried there, even though there were no gravestones. Apparently, the Indians did not approve of marking their burials. We also looked at the bell tower that was visible from the cemetery. The sign Mark read said that the uppermost bell of the tower was made of wood. All mission bells were wooden until bronze bells were created.

Then, we went into a place with tallow vats. Beef was melted and purified in the vats. What I was surprised at was that the vats were not very deep, like most of the tallow vats we had seen before. They were really quite shallow. In a short time, we had left the tallow vats.

After that, we went into the sacristy. I do not know how to pronounce sacristy. What happened is Mark took a picture of the sign, and he told me to write down what room we were in. I decided to ask Mishie what we were in here for.

Mishie said, "The sacristy and the smaller 'contra,' or secondary sacristy, were used by the Padres to prepare for church services, and to store items needed for the mass." I thought she sounded like a talking computer. It was pretty funny.

Inside the room, there was a sacristy chest, and something I don't know the name of. It looked like a cross on a pole.

The next place we went was the church. There was a confessional in the back and the walls were decoratively painted. As always, the altar was beautiful. I thought there was a shell painted on a wall. But, I wasn't sure. It could be a fan or just a fancy design.

I noticed that there were no pews in the church. There were no chairs, either. As a matter of fact, there wasn't anything that the people who came to mass could sit on at all! Just the bare floor!

"Mishie," I said, "When people come to mass here, do they have to sit on the floor?"

"What people?" she asked.

"The people that come to mass! Don't they have church services at all of the missions?"

"Except two," said Mishie. "The missions that are State Historic Parks, like this one, don't have people coming to mass at them."

"You said there were two. What's the other one?"

"Mission San Francisco Solano (Sonoma). At Mission Santa Cruz, there's a separate building that is a State Historic Park down the street from it, but the mission itself is not a State Historic Park."

I said, "Okay."

We walked around the church a little more, and then we decided to leave. Mark has forced me to include some facts about the church. Fun Fact: The walls of the church are four

78

feet thick! Other Fun Fact: In mission days, the church could hold up to 1,000 Indians! Other Other Fun Fact: Father Mariano Payeras, a priest that used to be at the mission, is buried under the altar! Other Other Other Fun Fact: Mark is a nerd!

Shortly after, Mark, Mishie and I went inside the soldiers' barracks. There were many beds, and above each one of them were a rifle, a bag, a rope, and some other things I can't identify. Also in the room was a table with benches on either side, and spears on a rack in the far corner of the room.

Next, we went into the corporal's apartment. In the first room, there were two tables. In the second room, there was just a bed. Some garlic was hanging from the wall. Mishie said that they believed garlic chased evil spirits away. I wish garlic chased evil Marks away.

Afterward, we all went outside to the patio. Mark, Mishie and I saw a barbeque, some picnic tables, barrels, pots, and pans. There was even a beehive oven. Mishie said that the patio was the place where the Indians cooked, made soap, carded wool, and lots of other things.

We went back indoors and soon found ourselves in the soldiers' apartments. There were beds, tables, and a fireplace.

Then, we visited the candle-making room. In this room, they made candles. Pretty obvious, right? In the room, there was a machine that looked like a rack. The machine dipped the candles into tallow, a product made of animal fat, and when they were done, the candles were hung to dry.

After that, Mark, Mishie and I went inside the master weaver's apartment. There was a bed and what looked like a spinner. (Well, of course there was a spinner...after all, it was the master weaver's apartment!)

Soon, we had left the master weaver's apartment, and we were on our way to the mayordomo's apartment. A mayordomo was the ranch manager. He was responsible for the mission's livestock and farms. So, his room was larger and more elegant than the past ones we have been seeing. His bed had a clean white canopy over it. It was really cool. And he even had his own kitchen! In the kitchen, there were pots, pans, plates, bowls, food, a stove, an oven, and more. It was really neat.

We went outside again and looked at the olive mill and press. A blindfolded burro or mule pulled a stone wheel to crush the bagged olives so they could be used for olive oil.

When we came back inside a few minutes later, we found ourselves in the weaving shop. Weaving looms were everywhere. There were also lots of spinners. On a table was a basket of wool. It looked so fluffy and soft.

We walked down to the next building. Mark took a picture of a bell hanging above the entrance. After searching for the Golden Mission a short while, Mark, Mishie, and I decided to see what was in the next room. When we got inside we were all confused. Why? Because it was a church. As you know, the three of us have already been inside the mission's church. Why would this mission have *two* churches? When I asked Mishie this, she laughed.

"I thought you guys would have figured out that *this isn't a church* by now. It's a chapel!"

Anyway, we started exploring the chapel. It was like and unlike the church in many ways. For instance, the chapel also had a confessional in the back. The confessionals looked exactly the same. But, the altar was different. There were three niches in the adobe, and a statue was standing in each one. There were also some candles beneath the statues. Unlike the church, the chapel didn't have Fourteen Stations of the Cross pictures in it. Instead, there were fourteen wooded crosses nailed on the wall.

In a few minutes, we had exited the chapel. Mark, Mishie and I decided to go through a tunnel. At the other end of the tunnel, we saw something that looked like it might be an oven. It might've been a barbeque. I don't know what it was, but it was sure neat.

After that, we all went inside the pottery shop. Red-orange pots were being displayed on tables and shelves. Pots were everywhere.

After we were done examining the pottery shop, we all went to the leather shop. Many leather items were in there, such as saddles, belts, handbags, and shoe molds. (I thought the shoe molds were really cute. They looked like something elves would wear. I mean, the ends were all pointing up!)

The room we went in next had a bunch of cowhides in it. The hides were displayed on shelves, and on the wall.

Then, we went inside an unfinished room. There was nothing in it. The sign that Mark read said that they left this room unfinished so that visitors could see how the original and reconstructed walls are bonded together and reinforced with modern concrete.

We were about to move into the next room when a large group of three or four–year–old children bounded in. Some harassed–looking supervisors slowly walked in behind them. We did not move into the next room because the kids were running around and screaming like a big flock of chickens when an angry lion is chasing them.

Mishie decided that we should go outside some more. "There's still some mission out there." Mishie said. "Besides, we'd need to go out anyway."

Outside, the first thing we saw was the fountain. Mark read the sign, and he said it was a gravity flow fountain.

We walked a little more, and soon saw another fountain. This one was a different design. I won't explain it very well, but I'll say it was kind of in a circle. I liked this fountain a lot.

Close to the fountain was, I think, a vat. It looked like a swimming pool. Off–topic thing I feel like saying: I want to go swimming now!

Mark, Mishie and I walked some more. We wanted to find the lavanderia. After going to the right some, we finally found the lavanderia. The design was a lot like the circular fountain. We checked out the lavanderia a bit more, and then went to the Indian apartments.

When we got to the Indian apartments, Mark and I were surprised to find just ruins. All it was was a lot of adobe bricks on the ground.

Next, the three of us went into the girls' dormitory. Young Indian girls 11 or older that were not yet married were brought here to learn how to sew, cook, spin, and weave. In the room, there were a lot of blankets on a long wooden bench. That must have been where the girls slept. There was also a table set with food and plates. My favorite thing about this room was that the windows were triangular. It was awesome.

Mark, Mishie and I went back to the part of the mission we had neglected. Now, the three and four–year–old children had left, and we could continue our tour.

The room we stopped at was the living room for the padres. The two padres received visitors and guests in this room. Sometimes, members of the Chumash tribe would come here to show their traditional songs and dances.

After that, the three of us entered the dining room. There was a *gigantic* table in the center of the room. I say it is 10 feet long. There were also some cabinets around the table. In the cabinets were plates and cups.

Afterward, we went inside the priests' room. There were two beds, one for each priest. There was also a chair and a desk for them to do their work in.

I was looking at the pattern on the blanket on the bed when the next room caught my eye. In front of me was the fanciest couch I had ever seen in my life. It was striped red and yellow, and had wooden armrests.

I walked right out of the room and into the priests' office and library. I thought it was weird because the couch was nothing like the rest of the room. The couch looked new and clean, but the rest of the room was old–fashioned and dusty, the way you would expect an old mission to look. New and clean and old–fashioned and dusty didn't really go together. At least, that's what I thought. Mr. Opposite Mark said the new couch, old desk, old bookshelf, and old photos had a *magnificent effect* on the room. What the heck does that mean? Wait... I know! It's Mark Language! I decided to ask Mark about it anyway, just to annoy him.

"What do you mean by 'magnificent effect'?"

"It looks cool," he said.

"Why did you say 'magnificent effect' when you could have spoken English and said, 'It looks cool.'?"

"Because I like to expand my vocabulary and be smart, unlike my sister, who is quite dumb."

That was when the conversation ended.

The next place we went was the community kitchen. There was a beehive oven, a table, a stove, and lots of different kinds of foods hanging from the ceiling.

We walked a little more and ended up in the granary. Here, wheat, corn, and barley were crushed. The thing that mashed the wheat, corn or barley looked a lot like an olive mill.

After leaving the granary, we went outside and gazed at the turkeys, chickens, and pigs. First we saw the turkeys. My favorite was a white one that was all puffed up. He was simply beautiful. The area around his eyes was blue, and the rest of his head and neck was red. He had fluffy, clean, white feathers all over except for the small parts where his feathers turned deep ebony. He paraded around the pen as if he was in a turkey fashion show. All the other black turkeys were acting regularly. In the next pen, there were some chickens. All were black. The last animals we saw were the pigs. There were two of them, strolling around in the pen. One of the pigs put its snout in the dirt, and started walking around the pen, oinking along the way. It got its snout dirty, but we all thought it was funny.

It took a while for Mark, Mishie and I to leave the pens. After a long time, we went to a place that had some Indian huts. We went inside each one, (except for the one that was being repaired), and I sat on a tree stump that was set near the pile of firewood. Mark and I searched for the Golden Mission a bit more, and then we decided it was time to leave the Indian huts and go to the mission blacksmithing shop.

At the blacksmithing shop, we saw many metal items including hammers and nails.

Mark, Mishie and I flew back near the entrance of the mission to see its hospital after looking at the animals some more and after passing an herb garden. In the hospital, there were many beds and many different kinds of medicines and herbs on the shelves. Garlic and other types of plants hung from the walls.

    In a short time, the three of us were standing outside the exit of the mission. Mishie pulled us upward with a faint, "Come on!" and our feet lifted off the ground.

Favorite Things at Mission La Purisima

1. There were lots of **animal** pens in front of the mission. I saw pigs, horses, cows, sheep, chickens, turkeys, and a very large ox with dangerously curved horns. It was in a pen of its own; you can guess why.

2. We went outside and looked at a really cool, **circular fountain**. It looked like a donut. In the middle of the donut, there was a fountain. I liked this fountain because of its great design.

3. In the girls' dormitory, there were **triangular windows**. They looked awesome!

4. In the priests' office and library, there was a **gold and red striped couch** that looked really cool. It looked very soft, and I wanted to sit on it.

5. In the leather shop, there were **shoe molds** that were really cool. I liked them a lot because the ends were kind of pointy.

6. After touring the chapel, we saw this **tunnel** that was really neat. We went under it a couple of times, and when I yelled, "MARK IS A NOODLEHEAD!" it echoed and Mark was embarrassed and annoyed. That is my goal in life; to embarrass and annoy Mark.

Mission Twelve

Mission Santa Cruz
(Founded: 1791)

Santa Cruz, CA

The Hard-luck Mission

Twelfth Mission: Mission Santa Cruz

*W*e landed in front of the mission. Or somebody's house that was designed to look like a mission.

"Is this a mission or someone's house?"

"Why would I bring you to a house?" Mishie asked me.

"I don't know… it just seems too small to be a mission."

"Well, it's a mission all right, but I can understand why you'd think otherwise. You see, the real mission collapsed in 1857 due to many earthquakes. Then, a much smaller replica of Mission Santa Cruz was built here." Mishie pointed to where we were standing, in front of Mission Santa Cruz. "The actual mission stood over there." Mishie pointed to Holy Cross Catholic Church, a church near the mission.

"So the church over there was part of the mission?" Mark gave me the heck-no look, and I gave him the it's-not-my-fault-you-don't-understand-me look. Whatever!

"No," said Mishie. "When the mission was ruined, they built that church, and as I said, built the replica over here."

Mark stuck out his tongue at me. He is a noodlehead. "Phhhhhtttt!" to you too, Mark.

First, we went to the State Historic Park down the street. It wasn't open, so we just looked at the building. It was made out of adobe and sticks. And probably mud, too.

Next, Mark, Mishie and I walked into the church. The thing I liked most about this church was the Fourteen Stations of the Cross. Instead of paintings, which are what we usually see at missions, there were small wooden crosses pinned on the walls along with words describing what happened in that Station. For example, Station I was 'Jesus is condemned to death.' The altar was pretty simple, just three niches with statues in them, and one very fancy niche that had plants and a model of a building in it.

After that, the three of us decided to go outside and read the plaque that was across the street in a park. It told the basic story of Mission Santa Cruz. I didn't want to read the sign, but Mark said I *had* to read it, so I pretended to read it and occasionally said, "Interesting," or "How magnificent," or "That's cool," or "That bit of information could *really* help us find the Golden Mission!" or "Wow, really?" Since I was saying something about every two seconds Mark probably figured out I never actually read the plaque.

Now, our trio was ready to go inside the mission. Mishie said, "Mishie service," even though you only had to make a donation. The mission was really small, so the gift shop was in the same room as the museum! In the first cabinet, there were vestments and a bucket thingy used for holy water.

"Vestments," said Mishie, "are those things." She pointed to some clothes that looked like long vests. They looked like they had been made out of really expensive material.

The second cabinet held books from the mission, hand-made nails, candles, and more vestments. Of course, weirdo Mark smiled at the books.

The next cabinet had a painting of the mission before it was destroyed set on top of it. There's nothing much to say about this cabinet except that it was a lot like the one before it. It had candles and vestments.

After that we looked at a painting of Justiniano Roxan, an Indian that was said to have lived to age 123. Wow! Other things in this cabinet included vestments.

Cabinet number five had a very graphic crucifix in it that was scary to me along with some…vestments.

The mission garden was my favorite part of the mission. You would walk down a path to the middle of the garden, and there was a fountain with either koi or goldfish in it. We're not sure which, but we think they're koi.

After awing at the fish, we looked around the baptismal. I noticed a roof structure over it. Mishie was almost completely sure that it was built to preserve it. The baptismal was all white and had cracks on it every now and then. That's because it was the original baptismal that used to be in the church.

There was also a statue of Father Serra in the back and a wooden carving of an Indian made by an artist in San Juan Bautista.

Mishie flew us over to the back of the Holy Cross Church. There was a piece of a rock wall being preserved there. For more details, look at the <u>Favorite Things</u> section at the end of this chapter.

The last place we went was the State Historic Park. The *mission* isn't a State Historic Park, like La Purisima and San Francisco Solano, but this building down the street is. It is the last original building left of Mission Santa Cruz. Outside, there were some giant redwood trees. One had a hole in the trunk. I stuck my hand in the hole, but didn't find the Golden Mission. Also there was an old wagon, picnic tables, and a beehive oven.

The first room had 160-year-old adobe in it (Geez!) and some things found in the ruins of an Indian house. This means a broken piece of ruler, marbles, shells, china bowls, yeah – you get the idea.

Then, we went to a room with Indian tools in it, such as bows and arrows and spears. There was also a humongous model of the mission before the earthquakes. It was really big.

Afterward, we walked into a room with benches facing a television. Funny thing is, the TV was covered up with a green piece of cloth.

Room number four had nothing in it. I think construction workers are working on an exhibit or something.

The fifth room had a wool swing and a bed inside it. There were also shelves with food on them, pots, pans, and a ladder.

Next, Mark, Mishie and I looked inside the next room, where there was a blacksmithing exhibit, a tool–making exhibit, and a herding, tallow–working, and weaving exhibit. It was okay.

The last and seventh room of this structure was the home part. Families lived in this room. It was kind of confusing, so I don't have much to say.

"I think we're done," Mark said.

Mishie nodded and said, "You're right. Come on."

"Let's go to a restaurant," I said.

"Which one?" Mark asked grumpily.

"Why are you so moody today? We need to cheer you up."

The moment I said those words, Mishie yanked us up into the air.

"Where are we going?" I asked.

"Get-cheered-up land."

"Get-cheered-up land? I've never heard of a place-"

"Just be quiet, and wait."

It didn't take long to get to the Santa Cruz Boardwalk. I got a hot dog, and Mark did, too. I didn't look at what was there until I finished eating.

"Mishie…" I was really surprised. I thought she only took us to missions. "You took us to an amusement park?"

"Yeah," she said. "We had time to spare, and Mark needed to be cheered up."

"Well, I've got to say. That was a really good idea!" I looked at Mark and continued speaking. "Hey, scardey-cat! When you're done eating your food, let's go on the rollercoasters. And that!"

I pointed to the "Fireball," one of those rides that swing you up in the air. I shouldn't have suggested that, because Mark went on it right after eating his hot dog, and he… um… regurgitated it.

Aside from Mark puking, the boardwalk was great! We had lots of fun, and I went on the rollercoasters a lot. There weren't just rides, either. There were games, and shops. But mostly, I just did the rides. It was sooooooo fun! If you go to Santa Cruz, and you like amusement parks, don't even think about not going here. Just go!

After a day of 3 missions and 100 rides (approximately) on the Hurricane (a fun rollercoaster), I was exhausted. I didn't even care that Mark and I were in the same bed and I had a nightmare that he beat me in a wrestling match! Today was spectacular!

Favorite Things at Mission Santa Cruz

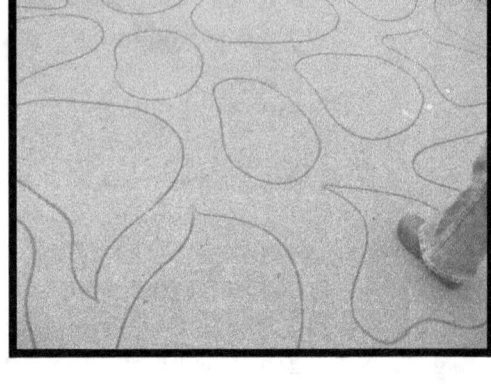

1. Outside the mission, there is a **sidewalk** that has a lot of cool shapes on it. I really liked the shapes.
2. On the **bell tower**, there was a lot of **moss**, but only on one side. That's because the sun only hit the other side of the tower.
3. When we visited the mission garden, we saw a **fountain with fish** in it. We're not sure if they were koi or goldfish, but we really enjoyed them.
4. Inside the gift shop, there were these little **angel pins** that had your **birthstone** on it. Unfortunately, I only found my dad's and my grandpa's birthstone, but they were still super cool.
5. Inside the church there were **Stations of the Cross**…but not just any Stations of the Cross. These Stations were words, not pictures. There was a wooden carving of a cross and then words describing the Station underneath it.
6. Behind Holy Cross Catholic Church, (the mission used to stand where this church is now) there was a small **wall of rocks and rubble**. This is a little bit left over from the mission. It was being carefully preserved.
7. The **roof** at the **State Historic Park** was really awesome, because it looked like it was made out of twigs and mud, the way the mission's Indians would have done it. I thought this was pretty neat.

Mission Thirteen

Mission Nuestra Senora de la Soledad
(Founded: 1791)

Soledad, CA
The Lonely Mission

Thirteenth Mission: Mission Soledad

"*W*e're almost there," said Mishie.

"Seriously?" We were flying over what I think was, uh, farmland. I saw rows and rows of plants, and I'm pretty sure a mission wouldn't just be standing smack dab in the middle of a farm. "You're kidding me."

"Am not! Look, there it is."

Believe it or not, Mishie was right. Well, it wasn't in the middle of a farm, because the plants stopped. But, the old mission looked pretty deserted.

We landed on the side of the mission, and we started to walk around. We saw a statue of Father Junipero Serra and what I think was a barbeque.

The three of us explored a little more and found this cross that had moss growing all over it. It was really cool. Moss on the cross! He, he!

On the left side of the chapel, there was also a very nice bell. I liked it because it wasn't in a bell tower, it was just hanging on the side, and this was unusual.

Then Mark, Mishie, and I walked over to an El Camino Real bell. Unlike most of the bells, it had a sign on it. Mark told me to write down what it said. It said, in 1906, guidepost bells were placed along the El Camino Real to guide early travelers and to preserve this historic route that linked California's missions beginning in 1769.

On our way to the entrance, we had to stop because Mark saw a sign he *had* to read along the way. It said that the founding date of the mission was October 9, 1791, and the restoration date was October 9, 1955. Mark found it very intriguing that they were both on October 9th, but I really didn't care. I was more interested in finding the Golden Mission.

Along the sides of the path were flowers, orange trees, and all different kinds of plants. We also noticed a not active fountain. It all was really beautiful.

After getting a map from a table, we strolled into the gift shop. You only had to make a donation, so there was no Mishie service. We went right into the museum since it was connected to the gift shop.

The first room was the prehistoric period room. It had lots of Indian tools and things in it. I especially liked the baskets, dolls and toys.

The second room was the mission period room. There was the original mission bell that was cast in Mexico in 1799, a big pot-like thingy that was used for dipping candles in tallow, and a mannequin of a padre dressed in an authentic robe. The padre was about the size of a 4th grader. I guess this explains why the doors at the mission are so short.

The third room was the rancho period room. There was a piano, robes that priests wore, and a model of the mission made by a person named Buddy Guzman. The thing I really liked about the model was that it looked like it was made out of wood.

The last and final room was the USA period room. There were models of the missions. We looked at the ones we had already been to, and the ones we were about to go to. There was also a sign-in book there. I signed myself in as "Allison," and signed Mark in as "Noodlehead." Now everyone who reads the sign-in book will know he is a noodlehead!

Then, we went back outside to where the church used to be. But, due to a past flood, the church had collapsed. Nobody ever got around to rebuilding it.

It's the mission custom to bury important people (probably fathers, brothers, or reverends) in the church. We saw their gravestones when we looked at where the church used to be.

We walked down a path that led us to a sundial, and then we came to a fountain. It was filled with small orange fish. It really reminded me of the giant koi fountain in Mission San Juan Capistrano. Mark, Mishie and I all thought this fountain was really cool.

Next, we went off to see where the old grist mill used to be. Then we looked at the adobe walls left from the blacksmith shop, carpenter shop, and Indian workshops. I really liked looking at them because I could use my imagination. One looked like Mark sleeping on his back. I pointed this out to him.

"Hey, that one looks like you!"

"No, it doesn't," he said.

"It does! Look, there's your head, and that's your nose. You're lying flat on your back. And behind your head, there's a giant fish popping its head out of the water about to eat your hair."

"I don't see that," he said. "But, that one looks like you when you're taking a nap."

"I don't take naps!" I told him.

"Yes you do."

"Okay, I used to. When I was three!"

"You still are three."

"I'm not three, I'm ten!"

"Well, you act like you're three."

I was having a little trouble thinking of something smart to say, so I used my backup backup. "You are such a noodlehead!"

Mark knows when I say this I've basically run out of good insults, so he just stops and pretends he's won the argument. He really hasn't though, because the one to quit talking is actually the loser.

Then, we went in a tiny room with a bazillion statues in it, which led to the church… wait… the *chapel*.

Well, the chapel was pretty simple. There were rows of benches, and an altar with a very large niche in it. In the niche, there was a very large statue of Our Lady of Sorrows. She is wearing black lace. My favorite things about the chapel were the awesome chandeliers hanging on the ceiling.

Mishie felt like giving out some information and getting Mark to take notes, so she said, "Did you know that this mission used to have mass 2 times a year? Thanks to a few great people in the community who arranged for visiting priests, they now have mass the first Sunday of the month as well as Christmas Eve and Easter morning, as long as a priest is available." This didn't work, so Mishie tried again. "And the Stations of the Cross in this chapel are original." *That* didn't even work. I was really surprised. Mark would usually be taking lots of notes by now. But he wasn't. So, Mishie tried one last time.

"This mission was known to have lots of bad luck. It was the 13th in the chain of 21, but I think that's just a coincidence. As you know, the number 13 is thought to be unlucky. It is known that brushwood shelters were built at first and that it was six years before the mission even had an adobe chapel with a straw roof.

"Not many priests like to stay at this mission because of the strong winds in the afternoon. In the 44 years that the mission was working, nearly 30 priests had come and gone." Mishie ended her 44 year speech with a huge smile. Mark smiled back at her, said thank you, and started writing. He wrote 10 pages all about Mission Soledad.

At first, I was having a hard time figuring out why Mark didn't just take notes in the beginning. Then it hit me. He wanted to wait, because he knew that Mishie would give out LOTS of information if he acted as if he didn't care about the little tidbits.

We exited the chapel, and stood outside the mission.
"Ready to go, guys?"
Mark and I nodded. "Yeah," Mark said.
Mishie smiled, and counted to three. Then we were off.

Favorite Things at Mission Soledad

1. There was a cute, black **cat** strutting around the mission. I thought he (or she) was adorable!
2. In the back of the mission we saw a **cross** in memory of somebody. There was **moss** all over it! The wood was practically green!
3. In the center of the cemetery, there was a **fish pond** with lots of small, orange fish. I really liked them.
4. After leaving the ruins of the blacksmith shop, carpenter shop, and Indian workshops, we noticed a **tree** with beautiful **flowers** on it. They were a light shade  of pink, and just…you have to see them. But we're pretty sure they only blossom around the spring.
5. To enter the chapel, we had to go through these really cool **doors**, with **wavy** designs on them. They were on the front entrance and the side entrance.
6. In the courtyard, between the fountain and the grist mill, there was a **tree**. It had **moss** on one side of it, and I really enjoyed it.
7. Inside the museum, there were **models of the missions** and a **mannequin** dressed up as a **monk**. He had no face, which I laughed at. I called him Mr. No Face Monk! They both were really cool!

Mission Fourteen

Mission San Jose
(Founded: 1797)

Fremont, CA

No Known Nickname

Fourteenth Mission: Mission San Jose

"*W*e're here," said Mishie.

"Huh?" Usually the flights were longer than this one. I looked down to see what was, without question, Mission San Jose. You could tell by the bell tower and white paint and cross on top of the building. Mishie pointed out that the bells in the bell tower were original.

Just to make sure we were in the right place, I pulled a map I always have out of my pocket. I looked at the mission we just completed visiting, Mission Soledad, and then found Mission San Jose on the map. This took a while, because I thought Mission San Jose was in the town of San Jose, which it wasn't. It was in Fremont. I eventually found it, though. The two missions weren't that far apart.

"Come on," said Mishie. "Let's go." She pulled us towards the museum, and we were almost inside the building when…

"Whoa! Hang on!" Mark yelled. "A sign!"

I sighed. "Mark, you have to break this habit! Reading signs wastes time, and we don't have all day. Every time you see a sign, you don't *have* to read it! We're here to look for the Golden Mission, not piddle around at these dumb signs! I mean, how is *reading a sign* going to help us? It's not like it has clues or something written all over it! Why do we need to know all about the mission, when we're just here to search for something? If we know the founding date, who founded it, special happenings, blah, blah, blah…is this information actually useful? No, not at all! *What is your problem?* You are just standing there, reading the sign, and all you care about is *it*. Not the Golden Mission, not me, not Mishie…just that sign! That's all you can think about right now, isn't it? *The sign?* Oh, my gosh! You make me soooo mad! You are just so…so…such a noodlehead!"

"Why, thank you," Mark said. Then he yawned a fake yawn. "That was a very good nap."

I suppose you want this translated from Mark language to English. Well, he meant that I was talking for such a long time, you could sleep while I was talking. Of course, this isn't true. I was only telling him the right thing to do, which only took about 10 seconds.

I sighed at him. I repeated the words, "You are such a noodlehead!" at him, and he responded with, "Why, thank you!" which is exactly what he said before. I then realized he was hopeless, and I gave up.

Mishie looked at us uncomfortably. "Uh…we were working our way to the museum?"

"Yeah," I said, and turned my back to Mark.

On our way there, I was still grumpy, so Mishie tried to cheer me up by giving me some facts. She should know by now this only works with Mark. Anyway, Mishie said to me, "In 1827, each side of the quadrangle was about 900 feet long." I ignored her, so she tried again. "In 1833, San Jose was the richest of all the California missions."

Just to make Mishie happy, I took out a notepad and wrote on it. I wasn't taking notes though; I was writing "I'm a noodlehead." Mishie thought I was actually taking notes, so she smiled and stopped talking. Then I erased "I'm a noodlehead," because I didn't have any tape to tape it on Mark's back.

The three of us went into the gift shop, which was the entrance to the mission. Mishie flew to the counter and said to the clerk, "Mishie service." Then we stepped into the museum.

In the first room of the museum, there was a display of Indians, a kiicha (a hut), and an arbor thingy that had grass on top. There were these little plastic (I think) Indian people, a little stick kiicha, and other things that Indians would have used or needed all in a glass case.

Other items used in the mission Indians' life were in glass cases on the sides of the room, like baskets, abalone necklaces, instruments, animal pelts, and there was a headdress that looked really fancy, too.

In the next room, there were photos of the mission being restored. It showed the progress of the building. I really liked that.

At first, I found room number three confusing. On the walls were these pictures of a gothic-looking church that was pretty, but I had no idea why it had anything to do with Mission San Jose.

I opened my mouth to speak, but Mark beat me to the question. "What is *that*?" he asked, pointing to the picture of the gothic church.

"It's rude to point," I said, sounding like Mom.

"Not if the thing you're pointing at isn't alive."

"It's still rude to point."

"I don't-"

"*That*," said Mishie, interrupting our argument, "Is Saint Joseph's Church. Also known as: the wooden church."

"I'm supposed to automatically understand that?" I asked. After an argument, I'm snotty to everybody, even my best friends.

"*No.* You're supposed to automatically listen to me."

"Sorry."

"One priest came to the mission and saw its buttresses. He thought they looked really weird. Buttresses are those big things of adobe or whatever that hold up the sides of a mission."

"Huh?" I asked.

Mishie quickly flew us out of the museum, and pointed at the buttresses on the side of the mission church.

"Those are buttresses."

"It's rude to point."

When we were back inside the museum, she said, "So, the mission priest thought the buttresses were ugly. He wanted them removed. So they removed them. And in a big earthquake, the mission came falling down. Now, that the original mission had crumbled, the mission priest decided to build a gothic-looking church in its place. They called it Saint Joseph's Church, in honor of Mission San Jose, since Jose means Joseph in Spanish." Then Mishie pointed at the picture of St. Joseph's Church.

"It's rude to point," I reminded her.

"Stop it!"

"Sorry, sorry, okay, okay…"

"Okay, so there's no more Mission San Jose. It's now St. Joseph's Church. They nicknamed the church 'The Wooden Church,' because it was made of wood. St. Joseph's Church stood for a long time. Over 100 years! Finally, they sold the old wooden church, and it was moved to San Mateo piece by piece. When St. Joseph's church was moved, they rebuilt Mission San Jose. So now we are at Mission San Jose, not St. Joseph's."

"And that's the 100 hour story of Mission San Jose…" I mumbled, not that happily. Mishie had been known to give out long and somewhat boring lectures.

"It wasn't that long," Mark said. Yeah, right! He's patient. I'm not. If he had the disability (it's not a disability, but I just call it that because that's what Mark calls it and he is mean) of being un-patient, he would be saying it was long, too!

We left the third room after Mishie's 100 hour lecture, and then we went into the fourth room. There was a piano in there – wait, no. My editor, Mark, says it's a *harmonium*. I see. Well, there was a *harmonium,* a neat wooden thing that I'm almost completely sure was a plow, some blacksmithing and carpentry items in a glass case, and a giant cauldron used for boiling annoying, noodlehead twin brothers. (Just kidding! But I wish I wasn't!)

The three of us wandered into the next room. There were Indian baskets, a papoose used to carry the Indian babies, some abalone, and weapons. In one glass case, there was a Spanish rosary, hat, and some cloth. There was also a bed, a chair, and a desk.

Room #6 had some more pictures of the gothic, wooden church and some more pictures of the original Mission San Jose. On a bulletin board in the back, there were a bunch of thank you letters to docents that gave some students a tour of the mission. They were are really sweet, and a couple were funny. You should read them if you go to the mission.

I really liked the vestment on the headless mannequin in the next room. There were also pictures of things that were used in the mission days, like bells, an organ, a doctor's kit, and a lamp.

In the room after that one, we saw Indian foods in glass cases, and a model of the church at Mission San Jose. It was really neat because it was like they cut off the front of the church, so you could see inside. It looked exactly like a mission church; there were little adobe (well, it was supposed to look like adobe, but if I remember correctly, it was paper) tiles on the roof and floor, and there were teeny little paintings and designs on the walls.

To make us laugh, Mishie went inside, and tried to go through the cut out doors. They were too narrow and too short for her. The doors went up to about her neck.

When Mishie looked up and noticed we weren't amused, she did a few cartwheels, something she is a master at. I looked at her with the you're-nowhere-close-to-funny-you-need-clown-lessons look, and she did two cartwheels in a row, which she is *not* a master at…so she fell on her butt…which made me laugh. Now she doesn't need clown lessons.

"This museum is big…" I said when we got into the 9th room.

"Yeah. You're right. I totally agree with you. You are so right. I can't agree more," Mark said.

"What? You sound sarcastic."

"I am," he showed me that there was no door leading into another room.

I sighed. Stuff like this always happens to me. I say that something is long, and there's the end of it. I say that something is short, and there's 20 more things of it. I say that I'm close to beating Mark in a board game and then…you get the idea.

The room we went into had a big blank spot on the wall. There was a big blue square on it, so I was pretty sure a movie of the history of Mission San Jose was supposed to play here.

"Hey, let's watch the movie! We could learn something!" I have a feeling you know who said this.

"Nah... I have a better idea. Let's search for the Golden Mission!"

"No! Watch the movie!"

"It probably runs every hour, and it's, like..." I looked at my watch. "12:34 right now. Do we want to wait for half an hour just to see some dumb movie?"

"Yes."

"You are crazy! Every time you see a movie presentation is going to start, you don't *have* to watch it! Watching movies wastes time, and we don't have all day! I mean, how is *watching a movie* going to help-"

"You know what?" he asked.

"What?"

"I don't want you to talk on and on forever again, so I've decided we don't need to watch the movie."

"Good for you!" I didn't mean this sarcastically.

Now that we had decided we were *not* going to watch the movie, we looked at the pictures on the walls a little. After two pictures, I noticed these were paintings of the California missions. I also noticed that we were exactly two thirds of the way done visiting them.

I looked around to see if there was anything else in the room. There was. At the bottom of the wall that had the big blue square on it, there were some models of the mission. None of them were store-bought, which made them really neat.

"We have some time," said Mishie. "Maybe, instead of watching the movie, we should go to lunch."

"Good idea," I said. "Let's eat at Subway."

"No, Quizno's!" Mark insanely likes Quizno's.

"Subway."

"Quiz-"

"Neither!" Mishie had just gotten upset.

We flew around aimlessly a little bit, and then I saw a Del Taco. We all agreed on eating there. When we were finished with our meals, we went back to the mission to complete our tour.

We picked up in the courtyard. There was a statue of Father Junipero Serra, and a fountain. The fountain was really shallow; not even half of it was filled with water. There were no fish in the fountain either…just a few coins.

Also, there were some graves in the courtyard, instead of the cemetery. I asked Mishie why they were there, and she said, "They ran out of room in the cemetery, so they had to put them in the courtyard."

I started to walk around and look at the few graves in the courtyard. There was a really big and fancy grave that looked sort of cool. I read the name on the grave and it said, "S. Higuera." Maybe S. Higuera had a lot to do with Mission San Jose's history!

Attached to the church were the remains of some walls. At their base, I noticed some squares on the ground that Mishie said used to be rooms attached to the church. The area where the gift shop is used to extend all the way to the church. I thought the outlines of the rooms were neat.

Don't get the triangular chunks of adobe walls on the gift shop side of the church confused with the buttresses. The buttresses are on the other side (main cemetery), are much larger, and a different shape.

Next, our trio went into the church. I noticed that the church was pretty large.

"Wow," I said to Mishie. "This is a big church."

"Yeah," she said. "The walls are 8 feet thick, the ceiling is 24 feet high, it's 125 feet long, and 30 feet wide…at least, it was in mission days. I'm not completely sure what it is now."

Anyway, the church was really pretty. There were balconies painted on the walls, which I found sort of surprising because I didn't notice this at any of the other missions. There was a very colorful organ in the real balcony, and it was yellow and blue and green, and just all sorts of different colors. I loved it!

As soon as I stepped inside, I saw the grave of Don Roberto Livermore. Whoever that is, he was probably important to the mission. I think being buried in the church is a great honor, so Don Roberto Livermore must have been a special person.

I also liked the candle holders in the church. They were under all of the Stations of the Cross, and they looked like little circular mirrors. When the candle was set on it, the candle would reflect on the little circular mirror. I thought that was a neat concept.

"This mission," said Mark, "only has twelve Stations of the Cross."

"Really?" I asked him. "Why?"

"I don't know. They just do!"

"Okay...well then, can you tell me why I counted fourteen, instead of twelve?"

"Because you can't count. You're three, remember? And you take naps. Three–year–olds can't count."

"I am *NOT* three, for your information. And I do *NOT* take naps. And there *ARE* fourteen Stations of the Cross. There are six on that wall, six on the opposite wall, and..."

"And that's it. There's twelve. Six plus six is twelve, three–year–old."

"I am *NOT* three! You need to listen to me and not interrupt! As I was saying, there are six on that wall, six on the opposite wall, and..." I paused for a dramatic effect. "two behind you, on the sides of the front door."

Mark looked behind him. There were two of the fourteen Stations of the Cross.

"Hey, I read in a book that there were only twelve!"

"Maybe the author messed up, and only saw the twelve on the sides of the walls, not the ones near the front door. Or maybe the two near the door were recently added. I'm sure lots of people make mistakes like that."

After a long time, we left the church and went into the cemetery. I noticed a skull and crossbones above the door that we used to get out of the church.

"Aren't those supposed to be above the entrance to the cemetery?" I asked.

"They are," said Mishie. "They're just on the cemetery side."

Anyway, we went to the cemetery and looked at the graves. Some were really big and fancy, like Thomas L. Smith's. Thomas L. Smith's was even fancier than S. Higuera's.

I also noticed a big post grave that had little specks of green on it. I have a feeling it was moss, and when I made sure I was right by asking Mishie, she said yes.

Then, I inspected the buttresses. They were like big rectangular blocks of adobe that were attached to the cemetery side of the mission church. I understand how they would help the mission stay standing during an earthquake. As long as the buttresses were strong, they could support the mission, so it wouldn't be falling down like London Bridge.

We took a short walk through the cemetery, but didn't find anything. After a while, we decided our tour was over.

On our way out of the mission, I started to think about the gothic church. Mishie says it was moved to San Mateo, just a little north of here, in little pieces. Well, it was once a part of Mission San Jose, so why wouldn't the Golden Mission be there?

Then again, if the Golden Mission had been in the church, when they moved it piece by piece, it would have been discovered. Unless it had a really good hiding place, or didn't even exist yet.

We were outside the mission. "Ready?" asked Mishie.

"Yes," Mark said.

"No." I said.

"No? Is it opposite day?"

"No, it is *not* opposite day."

"Then we're leaving. Come on! Off to the next mission! We're going to go!"

"Yes, we are. But not to the next mission. To St. Joseph's Church!"

It didn't take long to get there. It would have taken about 40 minutes to get there by car, and Mishie is super fast, so… I repeat, it didn't take long. It was only about 35 miles away from the mission.

The church looked exactly like it did in the pictures. Mark, Mishie and I wanted to go in, but it was locked. I doubt the Golden Mission was in there, anyway. We took a couple pictures, and then flew away.

"Allison," Mark said to me, "That was a waste of time."
"Yeah, right! It was a good idea!"
"No, it wasn't."
"It was!"
"Wasn't."
"Was!"
"Wasn't."
"Was!"
"Wasn-"
"I'm waiting for you to stop arguing," said Mishie. She reminded me of my mom, who says stuff similar to this a lot.
"Sorry," I said, and after a somewhat short pause, we started flying away.

Favorite Things at Mission San Jose

1. In the museum, there was a **bill of sale** saying that the **old wooden church**, St. Joseph's, had been sold for $1.00. Wow!
2. In the **courtyard**, there was a **fountain** that had very little water in it. It wasn't even half full. I still enjoyed looking at all the coins. I even put in a dime.
3. In San Mateo is the **old wooden church**. If you have time, you really should go there. But, it is about a 40 minute drive. The church could be locked up, but so what? At least you get to see it!
4. Above the entrance to the cemetery, there was a **skull and crossbones**. I liked it a lot.
5. Under each Station of the Cross, there was a **candleholder**. It looked like a circular mirror, so when you set the candle on top of it, it would reflect in the mirror and look really cool. Maybe people pray to the Stations at night, and there might not be any other lighting. Or it could be just a decoration.
6. On the **altar**, there were these **heads** that had no bodies. They were statues, not real human heads. I remembered seeing these at Mission Santa Clara, so I asked Mishie what they were, and she said they were supposed to represent angels. I laughed, and she said, "No, really!" so I guess heads on altars are meant to be angels (I still think this is very silly).
7. In the courtyard area, I noticed some squares on the ground that used to be walls for rooms. They were really cool.

Mission Fifteen

Mission San Juan Bautista
(Founded: 1797)

San Juan Bautista, CA

Mission of Music

CALIFORNIA MISSIONS (1769 - 1823)

- San Francisco Solano de Sonoma (1823)
- San Rafael (1817)
- San Francisco de Asis (1776)
- Santa Clara (1777)
- San Jose (1797)
- Santa Cruz (1791)
- San Juan Bautista (1797)
- San Carlos Borromeo (1770)
- Soledad (1791)
- San Antonio de Padua (1771)
- San Miguel Arcangel (1797)
- San Luis Obispo de Tolosa (1772)
- La Purisima Concepcion (1787)
- Santa Ynez (1804)
- Santa Barbara (1782)
- San Buenaventura (1782)
- San Fernando Rey (1797)
- San Gabriel Arcangel (1771)
- San Juan Capistrano (1776)
- San Luis Rey (1798)
- San Diego (1769)

Fifteenth Mission: Mission San Juan Bautista

*M*ishie pointed at Mission San Juan Bautista, the Mission of Music. "There it is," she said.

It was a rather nice mission, with a grassy field in front of it, and the small old–fashioned town of San Juan Bautista surrounding it.

"It's near closing time; we might have to hurry just a little."

As soon as we landed in the soft grass in front, Mishie tugged us towards the gift shop. That was the entrance.

"Come on! Come on!" she shouted. "Hurry up! Allison's right, Mark! You really are a slowpoke!"

I smiled. Suddenly, I was okay with Mishie rushing and pulling us around everywhere. Just as long as she insulted Mark, it was all fine!

We detoured to the left to see an El Camino Real bell hanging on an arch-like thingy. There were plaques there, too, and Mark read them quickly.

Inside the gift shop, they had really cool stuff that I wanted to look at, but Mark and Mishie said we had to go, go, go, so I didn't get to look at many things.

"Mishie service," said Mishie very quickly as we whizzed by the counter.

We opened the door to get out, when a white cat with brown patches from the other side of the door ran in. There's my favorite part of today.

I noticed a bunch of statues standing outside the gift shop. I think they were of saints or something.

We then looked into the courtyard. It was cool. Almost everywhere you looked you would see a rooster or chicken. They made lots of noise, which was kind of irritating, but I still enjoyed them.

Mark, Mishie and I strolled around the mission grounds more, and we saw incredibly neat plants, including a tree with a twisted up trunk. My favorite plant was a gigantic cactus that was probably four times as big as me.

After that, we went under some metal arches that had colorful Stations of the Cross on either side. I thought it was really awesome and original.

The Stations of the Cross were arranged in a backwards L shape, and at the corner of the L, there was the El Pozo, or Mission Well. I looked inside, but didn't find the Golden Mission.

We searched a bit around a wooden statue of Father Junipero Serra, and then we exited the garden.

Next, we went outside the mission and looked at a statue of Saint John the Baptist praying or something. This mission was named after him. San is Saint, Juan is John, and Bautista is Baptist in Spanish. He was holding his arms out, and had a pleading look on his face, so I'm almost positive he was praying.

We walked some more and soon found out that the mission was actually built on top of the San Andreas Earthquake Fault. Then we walked on the original El Camino Real road. It didn't have any pavement, just dirt. I could easily imagine this was how the road was in the olden days.

It was getting rather dark, *and* it had started to slightly sprinkle, so we decided to tour the parts of the mission that were inside the building.

First, we went to the museum. The first room had a video playing in it. It was a visual history of the mission. It showed how the mission was destroyed during the earthquake in 1906, and was later rebuilt. I thought this room looked like a small chapel. The things we sat in to watch the movie looked like pews, and there were paintings up front on the side of the movie.

The second room had adobe blocks with footprints in it – at least that's what the sign said. (Mark read the sign, of course.) I didn't see any footprints.

Next, we went into a room with an ***enormous*** model of Mission San Juan Bautista. The model nearly took up the whole room. We've seen a lot of models, but not models this large. You've got to see it.

The room after that held a glass case full of books. Mark worshipped it. He is sooooo weird! My favorite thing about this room was the money donation thing. It looked like you were dropping money down a well…or a pit. However you want to say it. I loved it! There was also a display of what a kitchen might have looked like, and Indian tools on display.

In room number five, we looked at blacksmithing items such as nails, saws, and bolts. Just like the previous room, there was a display of what a room might have looked like. This time, it was the living room. Mark, Mishie and I walked around a little and then decided to leave.

The last room of the museum held a rather big cross that stood in the middle of the room. But, I liked the gigantic chest of drawers more. The chest of drawers was really big, too. This is how big: you could fit a person in it. That's how big.

Afterward, we went to the church. This is the only mission with a 3–aisle church. I mean there were really three aisles. You would come in, and you would be in the center aisle. Then you would look to your left, and there's another aisle. Then you would look to you right, and there's another aisle. The main (center) aisle had an altar in front, and so did the other ones. But, the altar in the middle was the most fancy. The ones on either side of it were less fancy. (And guess what? The right and left aisles are identical! Neat!)

I saw some bottles in a round display case. Or maybe it wasn't a display case. It could have been a storage thing. But a sign said that there were holy oils in the bottles. The holy oils looked brownish-greenish, which was sort of icky, but it was still awesome.

I also noticed that under the Stations of the Cross they had the Station number painted on the walls with fancy designs around it. The designs were really cool.

My favorite thing about the church was the windows. They were stained glass, like most church windows, but they were checkered yellow and white. It was really pretty.

Then, Mark, Mishie and I walked into the cemetery. Nothing much. All it was was a bunch of crosses. No gravestones or plaques; just crosses. Oh yeah, and a super big cross. Mishie said that approximately 4,300 Indians, Spanish and Pioneer settlers were buried in the cemetery.

The last place we went was the chapel. It was a large room with a table in the middle, and pictures on the walls. There were chandeliers hanging from the ceiling, and big blue doors. There was a rather big hole in the bottom of one door, and Mishie said it was so the mission's cats could get in and out. They needed to catch mice. There was also a hole in the church's door, but it was plugged up.

Mishie also said that the wavy lines on the door represented the River of Life. She has mentioned this to us before, but I pretended I never knew about the wavy doors.

Mishie's last bit of information was that this chapel was once used as a basketball court. I thought that was pretty funny.

"All right," Mishie said. "We've gotta go now. Gotta get to the hotel."

"Gotcha," I said.

She pulled us up, and we flew to the hotel. We were asleep as soon as our heads hit the pillows.

Favorite Things at Mission San Juan Bautista

1. When we opened the door to exit the gift shop, an adorable white **cat** with brown spots scurried through. Sooooo cute!
2. Inside the chapel, there was a **door with a hole**, which let the mission cats through to catch mice. There was also one in the church door, but it was plugged up. The kitty holes were awesome!
3. We went out in the garden, and there were **roosters** walking around everywhere. Cock-a-doodle-doo! They really did start squawking.
4. In the garden, there was a **tree** with a really **twisted trunk**.
5. In the museum, there was a *gigantic* **model** of **Mission** San Juan Bautista. It was so big, it almost took up the whole room!
6. Also in the garden, there was an **enormous cactus**. It was probably four times as big as me!
7. In the museum, I saw a **pit** that you could throw **money** in for donations. It was really deep, and it looked like you were throwing your money down a well. I donated a dime and a penny.
8. In the church, they had **stained-glass windows**. They were checkered **white and yellow**, and they were really pretty.
9. Also in the garden were these outdoor metal **arches** that had the 14 **Stations of the Cross** on either side of them. What I liked most about these Stations was that they were awesome and original.
10. In the garden, there was a **metal gazebo** that you got to sit in. It was really cool, but the seats were wet because it had just recently rained.

Mission Sixteen
Mission San Miguel Arcangel
(Founded: 1797)
San Miguel, CA
Mission on the Highway

Also known as:
*The Un-retouched Mission

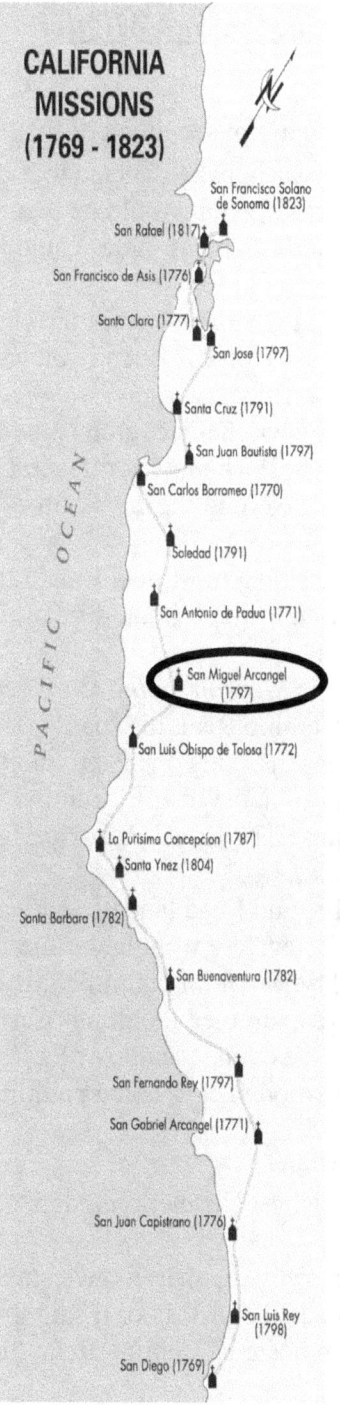

Sixteenth Mission: Mission San Miguel

I was worried that we might not see much of the mission because there was major earthquake damage to it on December 22, 2003. If nothing was open, it would be sort of pointless to come, right? So I asked Mishie if there would be anything to tour.

"Sure," she said. "Everything is open except the church, which is expected to be ready in 2010 or 2011. And you can only view the cemetery from the outside."

Mark said that Mission San Miguel's church is the best preserved of all the mission churches! The interior decorations of the church are just the way they were in the days of the Salinan Indians of 1821.

"There!" said Mishie. Mission San Miguel was in the small, off the freeway, town of San Miguel. I could've guessed that.

This mission's nickname is *Mission on the Highway* because it is right alongside El Camino Real, the road connecting the 21 California missions. This one is probably the closest to El Camino Real. (Bonus Fact: When El Camino Real is translated into English, it means "The Royal Road" or "The Royal Highway.")

Before long, Mark, Mishie and I had landed under a small archway in front of the mission. We went under the archway to explore the mission. Before going into the gift shop, which was the entrance, we examined the things outside of the mission. There was a beehive oven, a statue of Father Junipero Serra, an olive press, a wooden cart, and a painting of Mission San Miguel on a wall.

We went inside the gift shop.

"Mishie Service," said Mishie. The clerk nodded, gave us a map, and let us in.

Prior to visiting the Padres' living quarters, we stopped and saw a piece of tree bark outside the gift shop. It said the tree was carved with a cross to indicate El Camino Real, the

Royal Highway. In time, the tree healed itself and the cross was lost. When the tree fell down, the cross was found on the inside of the tree.

We looked at the courtyard from behind the ropes. In the center of the courtyard, we saw a fountain. Mishie said it was fed by a well.

Then we walked into a hallway used for shearing sheep in the summer. This place was called a "sheep gate." Since the hallway echoed, I decided to play an echoing game called, "Shout: 'MARK IS A NOODLEHEAD!' until he finally gets really mad at you." It's a fun game.

Finally, we walked into the Padres' living quarters through a door with a colored border around it. I forgot what color the border was, but all of the doors had a colorful border around them. Not all of them were different colors, but colors weren't repeated that often. The windows had neat borders, too. They were really unique, and the variety of colors looked really cool.

In one room, we saw another beehive oven, a stove, and some food.

Next, we went into the Padres' dining room. There was a table and some slanted shelves. The table looked very old and heavy. The floor tiles looked the same way. I noticed that the walls and ceiling looked old, as if they were original.

I asked Mishie, "This place looks...old. Is it original or something?"

Mishie nodded. "I guess you could call it original. The mission looks a lot like it did when it was founded. The inside of these rooms have never been repainted. And the pictures and colors you see are the originals painted by Indian artisans under the direction of Esteban Munras. Mission San Miguel is the last mission to have original paint."

After that, we went into the Padres bedroom. There was a bed, a chair, and a pair of shoes. Sheepskin was stretched over the windows because glass was too expensive and the sheepskin let light in also.

In the next room, the living room, we saw a pump organ made in Ohio. It looked really neat. We also saw some wool in buckets and candles hanging from the ceiling to dry. Mishie pointed out the display of ground minerals that were mixed with cactus juice to paint the walls of the church.

After strolling around the Padres' living quarters a bit more, we went back outside. Mark, Mishie and I noticed that the arches on the front of the mission were all different sizes. Mishie said they had planned to do this. Then I read the brochure to make sure Mishie was right. She was. The brochure said, 'Admire the original 12 arches and notice the planned variety of their shapes.'

Then we went back inside the gift shop. Since we had a little time to spare, we started looking at the various items for sale. Suddenly, a pleasant lady came up to us and said we could check out the temporary church if we liked. She told us that when we came out of the gift shop, all we had to do was knock on the first door to our right. I was really glad she was going to let us see it, because the Golden Mission could be in there, especially if the temporary church wasn't ordinarily open to public tours.

When Mark, Mishie and I happily came in, she told us that this wine vat/museum was being used as a temporary church. In thin glass cases were Fourteen Stations of the Cross. Usually, informative papers were there, telling people about the wine vats. The wine vat was decorated with flowers and lots of churchy things. A flowerpot covered a pipe where the wine flowed out. Then, she told us a story about the adobe brick floor tiles. When they were being made, and were outside drying, some big dog and cat decided to step in the tiles. Now, their paw prints are in the tiles. I really liked that story.

In about 15 minutes, we had exited the temporary church. We explored a little more outside the mission, and soon decided it was time to go check out the monument.

On our way there, I noticed that cactus was lined along the walls. Mishie had mentioned to us before that this mission was known for their cactus gardens, and I can now see why. I mean, we walked about 1,000 feet to see the monument, and there was cactus all along the way.

We finally arrived at the monument. It was a big reddish-brown bell tower. If you're driving on the freeway, you will definitely see it. The sign Mark read said that the bell tower was in memory of Father Fidelis Wieland, O.F.M. He was a former superior of Mission San Miguel.

In a short time, Mark, Mishie, and I were done touring the monument.

"1, 2, 3!" said Mishie, and we lifted up into the sky.

Favorite Things at Mission San Miguel

1. Since the church was being repaired, (There was a major earthquake on December 22, 2003!) a museum room with a wine vat in it was being used as a temporary church. A wonderful lady told me a story about why there are **animal prints** in the adobe **floor tiles**. It was a great story, and the animal prints were awesome!
2. Before going into the museum, I saw a **piece of tree bark** on display. A sign above it told the story of the **cross**. It was sooooo cool!
3. On the front of the mission, there were **twelve arches, all of different sizes**. They did this on purpose. I really liked comparing the big and small ones.
4. In the museum, there were no glass windows. Instead there were **sheepskin windows**, which I thought was cool. The sign Mark read said that glass was expensive, so the padres used sheepskin instead. It worked just as well!
5. To the left of the museum entrance, there was a **painting** of **Mission San Miguel** on the **wall**. It was really good; it looked like a professional did it! Wait…a professional probably *did* do it!
6. To enter the mission, we had to go under this very amazing **arch**. It looked old, and… I just liked it a lot.

Mission Seventeen

Mission San Fernando Rey de España
(Founded: 1797)

San Fernando, CA

* *Mission of the Valley*

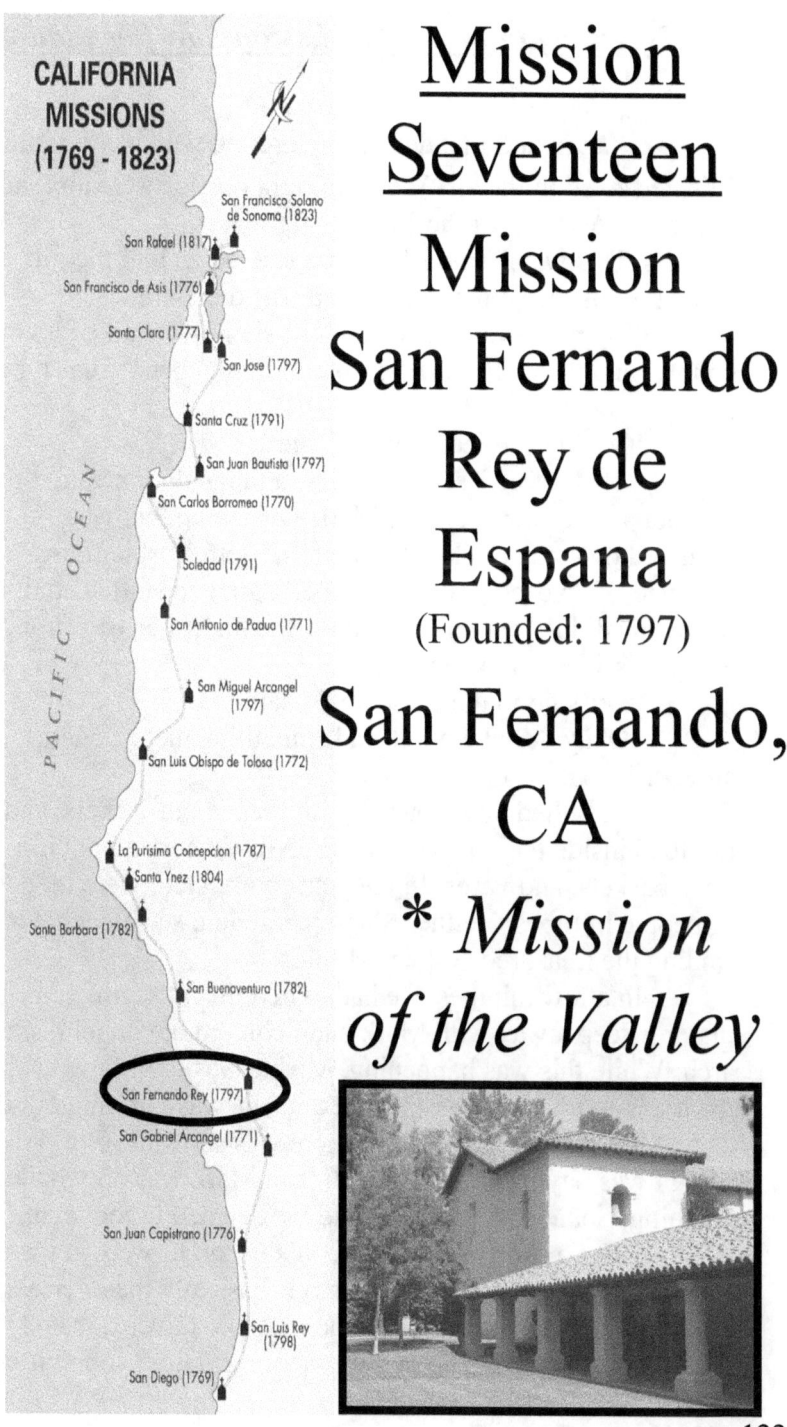

Seventeenth Mission: Mission San Fernando

Mark and I landed on the ground with a soft thump. Mishie stayed in the air. We were right outside Mission San Fernando, Mission of the Valley.

"This way," said Mishie, as she led us into the gift shop. At this mission, the gift shop was the entrance.

When we were inside the gift shop, we walked up to the counter and the clerk said, "Two children tickets? That'll be $6.00."

"Mishie service," said Mishie.

"That's free," said the clerk, and the door swung open. As soon as we were outside, Mark saw a map that was mounted on some bricks. We ran to it, with Mishie flying alongside. We each grabbed a paper map, and started studying it. Mishie didn't get a map because she knew her way around every mission that existed.

"Let's go to the museum," I said.

"Okay. Maybe we'll find something there," Mark agreed.

We pulled down our hats, tightened our jackets, and tip–toed inside the museum. There, Mishie pointed out old pots, baskets, and vases. In the next room, there were models of people in robes. Neither Mark nor I could see any clue to finding the treasured Golden Mission.

In a few minutes, we had exited the museum, and I was playing keep–away with Mark's tan colored hat under a small arch. While this was happening, Mishie was rambling on about the arch, and why it was so short and she was pointing out that part of the old adobe wall over there was showing. But, I don't think I was paying attention at all, and Mark was only half listening. So, Mishie gave up, and we decided to move on.

After a short walk, Mark, Mishie, and I were at the Mayordomo House. A mayordomo is basically the overseer of the mission. He is in charge of the mission's livestock and he supervises the Indians. When we went inside, we found it was a small, one-room house. On the right side were two beds, on the left side were two tables and in the middle was a model of a lady, cooking, on a stone stove. Mark noticed that there were coins on the beds. There was a single coin on the table, and a whole lot on the floor.

"Maybe it's a clue," he whispered. Yeah, right!

The next place Mishie led us to was the Convento which took 13 years to build. In the first room was an organ. Mark and I were both amazed. We walked into the next room, expecting something great. When we entered the room, a television was showing videos about each mission. Huell Howser was touring the missions and pointing out all of the important details.

Mishie left us so she could go see the rest of the convento. I don't know why she couldn't just stay and watch the movie with us, but she tends to be weird at times. But, I've noticed that everybody is weird at times (excluding Mark, who is weird all the time), even if they won't admit it.

"We might want to get that video," suggested Mark. "It might have some valuable information."

I shrugged. "We have enough clues by touring these missions ourselves. Who cares what Hue Houses has to say?"

"His name is Huell Howser! And I care what he has to say!"

"I didn't mean that literally. But, really Mark, if we bought that video, that'd wipe out our allowances for a month! It's probably, like, twenty dollars!"

"So? Mishie can use that thing where she says, 'Mishie service,' and we get something for free. That's how we get in each mission without paying. Mishie Service! Remember?"

"That just works on getting into missions. And I don't want Hue Houses's video!"

"Huell Howser!"

"I don't care, okay?"

"Gggrrrrrrrr!" Mark growls. It's very abnormal.

"Break it up, you guys!" Mishie had come back. "What are you arguing about?"

"I forgot," I said. "It was getting too intense."

Mishie sighed. "Let's leave."

After a walk with lots of glares from me to Mark, we ended up in the Old Mission Church. "It's very pretty," I said.

"Humph!" said Mark. He was still mad at me. It takes him so long to get over things.

But, I was right. The church is *very* pretty. So pretty, no adjectives can describe it. Maybe it was stunningly beautiful. Or it could have been magnificently splendid. Maybe I should just say it was amazing. Mishie told us that Pope John Paul II visited the church in September of 1987, and then we exited. Mass just ended and another one was ready to start.

When we were out of the church, and the argument was finally settled, we went into the Convento again. In the first room, there was a picture of each mission in a frame on the wall. Underneath that, there was a glass case that had tools that the Indians used.

Then, Mark, Mishie, and I went back into the room with the television. Mishie made Mark and me promise not to argue. (At this mission, at least) To make sure we kept our promise, Mishie stayed with us.

Next, we went into a room with lots of miniature statues. Mark and I enjoyed it a lot, but didn't see any clues whatsoever.

In another room, there were three wooden choir stalls. Mark sat in one, I sat in the other, and Mishie, since she was only about six inches tall, sat on the edge with what I thought were armrests far above her. I'm not sure if they were armrests, though. When I put my arms on them, my arms were about level with my shoulders.

Then we went in the next room, which had a place to store meat in it. I ran up a set of stairs, and forced Mark to take a picture of me. That's what you call fun!

Afterward, we visited the Bishop's Room. There was a bed, a trunk to put items in, and a sign that told all about it.

Soon, we all came into the library. It was filled with books, and Mark was eager to read one. But then, he saw that they were all in a foreign language. There were candlesticks on top of the bookshelves, and portraits of people hung on the walls. Mark said it looked great. I said it looked like a room. Mark is such a geek.

Next, we went into the Madonna Room. It was filled with Madonnas (figures of Mary). We all loved it. My favorite was one with Mary holding a baby standing in the middle of a field. There were children playing baseball around her. Mark said he liked this one too. (He's a big baseball fan, but I can't understand why. He really sucks at baseball.) There was also a figure I enjoyed of Mary holding Jesus but neither of them had faces, and Mary didn't have hair.

After that, we saw the Governor's Room. It was just like the Bishop's Room, only a tad bit fancier. Finally, we were finished with the convento.

We were getting hungry, so we took off for a quick bite to eat. Fortunately, the vote for the restaurant was unanimous, and we were eating at Subway.

"What's next?" I asked Mishie, after a wonderful lunch (Eat fresh!☺).

"Look at the map, dummy," Mark is evil. It would be quicker if Mishie could just tell us. I made that a point.

Mishie had settled the argument. I don't know how she does it. Our parents say we're impossible, but she obviously knows a secret about stopping fights.

"We're going to see a statue of Father Fermin Lausen," she said.

We looked at the statue of Father Fermin Francisco De Lasuen. O.F.M. He founded this mission. After walking a bit, we looked at a statue of Father Junipero Serra. He founded the first nine missions.

After that, we walked into a building that showed what a blacksmith's shop might have looked like, and it also showed a weaving loom with some of the products made. According to Mishie, the furnishings in here are original. Some coins were scattered on the floor and on things in the room. There was a piece of material on display that had probably, like, $1.00 on it (in coins). Mishie and I are having a hard time figuring out why this is the only mission with coins all over.

Soon, we took a look at the fountain outside. Clear water was streaming from the top. The fountain did look marvelous.

Last, we all went to the Bob Hope Memorial. There was a man–made stream in front, with a statue standing in the center. We strolled down the walkway, and soon found the tomb of Bob Hope. His wife had a tomb also, but she was still alive, so she wasn't in it. When Mark, Mishie, and I walked farther, we found the grave of one of Bob Hope's children. There were also other people's tombs that were related to Bob Hope in some way.

"Okay," said Mishie. "That's it."
"We're done?" I asked.
"Mmm–hmm,"
"So we can leave now?"
"Yeah,"
"All right, let's go!"
And we took off into the air once again.

Favorite Things at Mission San Fernando

1. When I was on my way to see a statue of Father Fermin Francisco De Lausen, there were some kitties behind a gate, having some cat food. Keep an eye out for cute **cats** all over Mission San Fernando.
2. A **dog** inside a closed building was guarding it, and when he was brought outside, he started jumping straight up in the air, and barking and doing all sorts of things. Make sure, if you can, to see the dog.
3. Inside the convento, there is a **library**. Mark is forcing me to make the library our third favorite, just because he liked it. But, I will admit it…the books are kind of cool…just kind of!
4. There were **coins scattered** at various displays throughout this mission! And I don't know why! They should nickname this mission, Mission of the Coins! Most of the coins were in the Mayordomo House and carpenter shop. The coins were neat. Look for them!
5. In the **courtyard**, there was a gigantic **fountain** with a really neat shape. I stuck my hand in the water, and it was nice and cool.
6. When we had exited the museum, I noticed that part of an **adobe wall** was exposed. I thought it looked really neat.

7. In the mission, there was a **pomegranate tree** that had big red pomegranates growing on it. Don't eat one, but they are pretty to look at!
8. No other mission has a **Madonna room**! San Fernando is the only mission with one! So, if you visit this room, check out the Madonnas. They are really unique, and make sure you pick out your favorite ones!

Mission Eighteen

Mission San Luis Rey de Francia
(Founded: 1798)

Oceanside, CA

King of the Missions

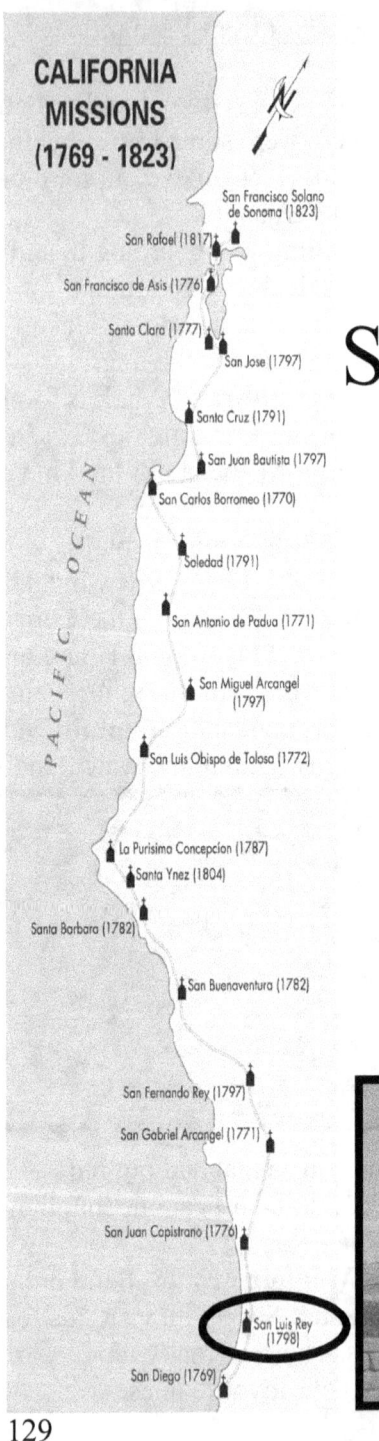

Eighteenth Mission: Mission San Luis Rey

"*T*here it is!" I shouted.

Right below us, was Mission San Luis Rey, the King of the Missions.

When we landed, we went inside the entrance. The lady asked, "Mishie service?" before Mishie could say anything.

"Yes," said Mishie.

The lady nodded toward the museum. "And no pictures inside the building," she said.

As soon as we were inside, we started examining things for clues, but we didn't find any. In another room, there were models of tools and baskets the Indians used.

When we had finally exited the museum, Mark, Mishie and I found that we were in a small garden. We walked down some to the left, and saw a model of the mission.

Next, all three of us went into the church. There were hundreds of statues all around, and they were really lifelike. The bloodiness of some of the statues scared Mark and me. Mark wouldn't admit it, though. Mishie just kept her eyes closed. I thought this was a good idea, so I kept my eyes closed, too. I later regretted this because Mishie told us outside that there was an original baptismal in there.

The next place we went was the cemetery. Once, we went off the path, and walked on the grass. It felt weird stepping on dead people. I thought I would share this with Mark, so I said, "Hey Mark, did you ever realize we're stepping on dead people?"

Mark didn't respond. I just ignored it because Mark usually doesn't answer me if I say something he thinks is dumb.

I kept walking. I didn't notice it at first, but it was very quiet. I don't like quietness, so I repeated what I had said before.

Mark didn't respond again. I looked around and realized Mark was gone! I remembered when he did this to me at Mission San Carlos, so I just said, "Come out, come out, wherever you are! I'm not going to look for you, because I don't care if you get lost!"

I saw some movement from behind a tree. Then Mark jumped out. He had his tongue sticking out and his eyes were crossed.

"I'm a dead person!" he said. "Allison stepped on me, so now; I'm going to step on her! Bwah-ha-ha-ha-ha-ha!"

Then Mark did a slow and terrible karate kick. He wasn't close to me, so I didn't even dodge it. "Now I have stepped on Allison and she is a dead person, too! Come with me to the world of dead people!"

"I don't think so," I said. "That was very immature of you."

"I think you got scared of it."

"No, I didn't."

"Whatever. You did."

"Be quiet."

Aside from stepping on dead people, the rest of the cemetery was great! There were beautiful flowers everywhere that people had placed on some graves, and on the memory wall. The flowers were colorful and probably smelled good.

The fountain in the cemetery was just gorgeous! It was in a...um...barbell shape. At one end was a fountain that shot out water in a straight line. It ran down a man-made stream, and then ended up on the other end, where water was bubbling up. It was very neat.

Afterward, we looked at a memory wall. I really liked the decorations on it. There was one with an artificial blue butterfly, and most of them had flowers. I was almost sure that the things on the wall were plaques.

"Mishie?" asked Mark. "What are those?" He was pointing to the plaques.

I looked at Mark with the you-don't-know-oh-my-gosh-you're-so-dumb-and-it's-rude-to-point look. He looked at me with the do-you-know-prove-that-you're-smarter-than-me look. Well, I was up to the challenge.

"I think I know!" I might've been exaggerating a little bit. I mean, I was waving my hand up in the air, and jumping up, like, 28 feet off the ground. "Those are PLAQUES! I'm sooooo smart!" Now, *that* was exaggerating. I hate to admit this, but Mark might be a *little* smarter than me. Just a little. Well, not really. He's smarter than me by…a long shot.

"Actually," said Mishie, "These aren't plaques. These are like doors." She tapped on one. She had said this at Mission Santa Barbara, when I said something similar to whatever I just said. "You open it up, and put somebody's ashes inside."

"Ashes?" I inquired. "You mean once you're dead, they burn you?"

"You have a choice. You can either be buried, or cremated." Mishie said.

"Cremated? What's cre-?"

Mishie sighed. "Cremated means, as you said, once you're dead, they burn you."

"Oh, okay…so, on average, are more people buried or cremated?"

Mark gave me the you're-off-topic look and I gave him the you're-a-noodlehead look. Who cared?

"I dunno…" Mishie looked confused. "That's not my department."

"Department? So you have your own little department for mission fairies, and then there's cremation fairies, and there's badminton fairies, and oohh! Noodlehead fairies! To deal with Mark! Say, Mishie, have you ever met a noodlehead fairy?"

"No…Allison, let's stop talking, okay?"

Subsequently, Mark, Mishie and I decided to visit the lavanderia. It was a place where the women washed clothes and bathed. The girls were naked, and the boys wanted to … well, look at them. To prevent the boys from coming in, or peeking, cactus was planted around the lavanderia. That'll keep them away!

We crossed the road, and soon were standing under the arch that led into the lavanderia. Mark and I eagerly skipped down the 45 steps, and looked at the two bathtubs. Each one had a gargoyle with a pipe for a mouth at the end. Water came through the pipe, and put water into the stone tub.

In a few minutes, we had finished our tour of the lavanderia.

After that, we all walked back to the mission. We wanted to see the ancient pepper tree. Supposedly, it was the first pepper tree planted in California. That's why it was called the, "Mother of all Pepper Trees."

But, some friars live at the mission, and the pepper tree was in the place where they live. The staff wouldn't allow anyone in, so the friars could have peace and quiet. That kind of sucked, because the Golden Mission could be with the friars, but I doubt it. One of those friars would be living in a mansion, not a mission right now. (Ha, ha! Do you get my joke? It's very good! I have good jokes, unlike Mark!)

We all looked at the pepper tree from outside the gate. There were long supports holding up the branches, and the tree was really big. I did the puppy dog face, but we still weren't let inside. (And I have a really good puppy dog face! It usually works!) But I'm not that sure they saw me. If they see you, you might get in. But only if you have a good puppy dog face like me.

After browsing in the gift shop, it was finally decided that we should leave. Our trip of this mission was short because lots of things were closed to the public. Still, I enjoyed it.

"Time to take off," said Mishie.

Soon, Mark, Mishie and I had risen into the air.

"Here we are," said Mishie. "The hotel."

"Yes! We're here! Finally! After hours and hours of flying! Yes!"

"According to my stopwatch, it only took near 10 seconds," said Mark. Did I ever say he was a know-it-all?

"Yeah, yeah, yeah! Just zip your lips and ignore the impatient me!"

"You're grumpy! You must be really sleepy!"

"I told you to ignore me! You're not a very good listener."

"I wonder why I get A's in school then. And if I'm not a good listener, you must be."

"I am."

"Then why do you get C's and occasionally B's in school?"

"Since when did we start talking about grades? You are a subject-changer!"

"Subject-changer? What kind of name is that?"

"A name describing you."

"Oh, my gosh! You need to think up better names to call me. The names you call me now aren't even insulting! Can't you come up with something better than 'noodlehead'? Or 'subject-changer'? Or 'wimp'? Or 'sissy'? I could fill a 200 page book with the dumbest names you've called me!"

"Oh, yeah? I could fill a 1,000 page book with the dumbest names you've called me!"

"You can't type that fast!" he said.

"I can't type," I said. "And why are we arguing about typing?"

He shrugged. "You started the argument. All the blame is on you."

"I did not start it! You started it off with that smart-aleck remark about me being impatient or it taking 10 seconds or whatever!"

"I totally disagree! You started it off when you said that the flight had taken forever, which it didn't!"

I sighed. "I give up on you, Mark."

I didn't notice it, but while we were arguing, Mishie had taken us up the stairs, into the room, and we had changed into our pajamas. I figured we were too busy arguing to realize what we were doing.

With slight difficulty, I fell asleep and had a dream Mark and I were arguing. But everything turned out okay because I dreamed that I won the argument.

Favorite Things at Mission San Luis Rey

1. There was a **skull and** crossbones over the cemetery. I thought it was interesting.
2. There was a **statue** with **no head** in a niche on the front of the mission church. I called him Mr. No Head. I thought he was funny.
3. In the center of the place where the friars lived stood a **gigantic pepper tree**, the tree was really big and really cool!
4. Everything in the **lavanderia** was awesome! I especially liked the steps leading to it, the gargoyle waterspout, the very deep kiln with a soda can at the bottom, and the cactus planted around the lavanderia. Plus, if the lavanderia is locked, then ask an officer or somebody to open it. Because you need to go see it!
5. In the **cemetery**, there was an awesome **fountain**! The water was super clean and I loved the stones that were at the bottom!
6. On the **door** used to enter the **church,** there was a **wavy design**. It looked really neat, and Mishie told us *again* that it signified the River of Life. I thought it was cool *again*.
7. To the left of the courtyard, there are **models** of **Mission San Luis Rey**. They look very neat.

Mission Nineteen

Mission Santa Ines

Solvang, CA
(Founded: 1804)

*Hidden Gem of the Missions

Also known as:
Mission of the Passes

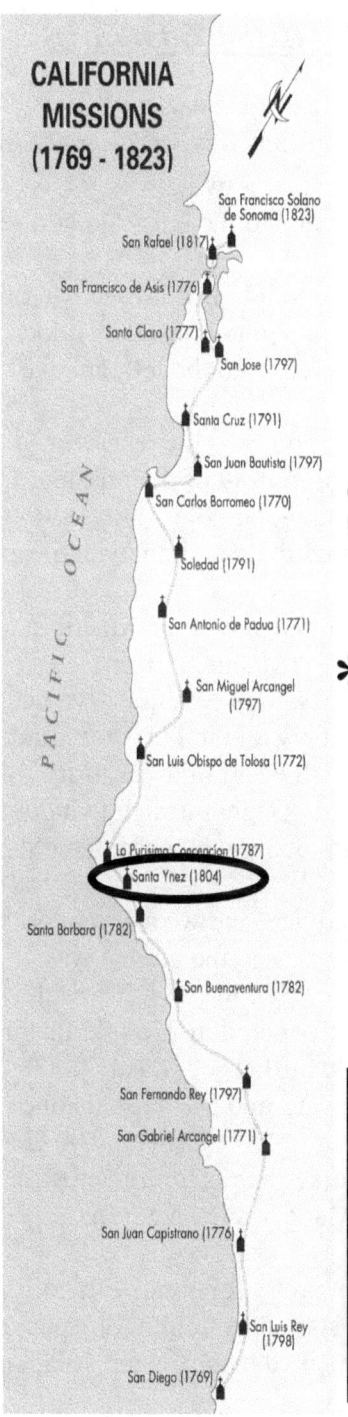

Nineteenth Mission: Mission Santa Ines

*W*e had left Mission San Luis Rey, and were flying over houses, trees, and roads when we saw it.

Mark nudged me and pointed to the left. "Do you see it?" he asked. "It's right over there."

I squinted my eyes. Sure enough, I could see what was definitely a mission. It was Mission Santa Ines, the Hidden Gem of the Missions. Mishie veered us to the left, and we landed right in front.

The first thing we checked out was the reservoir. It was easy to get to because it was right in front of the mission. I thought it looked like a deep rectangular hole.

Mark, Mishie and I entered the gift shop, which was the starting point of the tour.

The lady at the counter stared at Mishie. Mishie stared back. She looked kind of confused (Mishie, I mean).

"Say your thing," the lady said to Mishie. "I've been working here for a long time. I know all the fairy tour guides."

"Mishie service," said Mishie sort of awkwardly.

The lady nodded, and said, "Right through that door and into the vestment room. But you might want to go outside first. Looks like it's going to rain."

We decided to take her advice, and we all went outside into the cemetery and garden. Mark said the garden was one third of its original size, and from 1804 to 1834, it was the center of activity for a large ranch operation. He said that in 1812 the mission produced 3,400 bushels of wheat, 3,000 bushels of corn, 80 bushels of beans, and 514 bushels of peas. In 1820, the mission had 7,000 cattle, 5,000 sheep, 100 goats, 100 pigs, 120 mules, and 600 horses. I was impressed with all of this information, so I asked Mark where he got it.

"A sign," he said.

We walked up to a really pretty fountain with no fish, but a lot of coins in it, and then started examining the plants. There was this plant that I really liked in particular. It looked like a giant asparagus, except curly at the end. That plant was really neat. (It looked like the one at Mission San Juan Capistrano!)

We also checked out a model of Mission Santa Ines that was really unique. I liked it a lot because it sort of made the mission look like it was made out of bricks.

Then, Mark, Mishie and I walked under some kind of vine. It wasn't a grape vine, like they had at most of the missions; it looked like a vine holding giant peas in a pod. Mark said that they were probably vanilla beans. Do vanilla beans grow in a pod? And do peas grow on a vine?

At the end of the vine, there was a shrine that had a statue of The Virgin Mary at the end. She had bunches of flowers around her, which I thought was pretty. The flowers weren't growing there; they had been cut, and then placed there to worship her. There was also a sign that said she was also known as, "Our Lady of Lourdes."

After that, we saw the cemetery, which was pretty much just a bunch of neat crosses. There were some big ones and some small ones. Most of them were wooden, but there could have been a few that were stone.

Next, we walked down farther, and read a sign that said we were standing where the first institution for higher education in California was built. The school was called, The College of Our Lady of Refuge of Sinners. That's a very long name for a school!

Mark made a funny face. He obviously didn't understand something. "Isn't the first college in California at Mission Santa Clara?"

"Well…sort of," Mishie was about to explain something to us.

"This college was the first college to be **built.** Santa Clara is the first college still **operating** and the first **chartered** institution for higher education in the **new** state of California. Our Lady of Refuge of Sinners was **built** when California was still Mexican territory in 1844. California became a state in 1850. By 1850, Our Lady of Refuge of Sinners no longer existed. It was moved to Santa Ynez in 1846 (after 2 years of operation at Santa Ines), and then became known as Guadalupe College. To be recognized as an institution of higher learning in the **new** State of California, the institution needed to be granted a California charter. This honor goes to Santa Clara University, and Mission Santa Clara, which was built in 1851. A few weeks after Santa Clara received its charter, The University of the Pacific (a Methodist college) received its charter – making it the second institution of higher learning in the new State of California. They both still exist today."

Then we saw a statue of Saint Francis and the Wolf of Gubbio. It looked like a statue of a man who had his hand on a wolf. He was staring at the wolf and the wolf was staring at him. Mishie saw me looking at the statue, so she told me a cool story about it.

In a town called Gubbio, there was a wolf that kept attacking livestock and sometimes even people. The people were not happy about this, so they fought against the wolf, but some of the people were killed, and the wolf survived. So they called Saint Francis, who was thought to be able to communicate with animals. He talked with the wolf, who said that he had been abandoned by his pack because he had an injured leg, and couldn't keep up with them. He wanted to eat food like deer and rabbits, but he was too slow to catch them with his hurt leg. So he ate sheep instead. The shepherd tried to protect his sheep, so the wolf had to fight back to get the sheep. Then the villagers started a fight against the wolf, so he had to defend himself again. Saint Francis understood that the wolf was only hungry, so he made a compromise with the town of Gubbio. They would feed the wolf, and make him their friend, and he would not harm them.

After that, we all read another sign that told the story of Pasquala, a young Indian girl who saved Mission Santa Ines. When Pasquala became ill, she was tended at the mission until she was better. When she heard that the Tulares were about to attack the mission, she ran away to alert the priest. Pasquala warned the priest, and Mission Santa Ines was saved. Sadly, Pasquala died of a fever contracted when she made the difficult journey to warn of the attack. Legend says Pasquala is buried in the mission church.

We exited the garden and cemetery and went outside to a rose/cactus garden outside the mission. On our way there, Mark saw a sign. He read it out loud so I could learn too, even if I didn't want to. The sign was about Indians being separated into different groups for better instruction. Married couples and their children lived in the Indian village. Young women had their own section of the mission, and so did young men.

We arrived at the rose/cactus garden. The rose garden was planted in 1995 just to make the mission better. Part of the mission quadrangle used to stand where the rose garden is now. We went down a path. On one side were cacti, and on the other were roses. I liked one pinkish-yellowish rose in particular.

Before entering the museum, we stopped to look at the original 19th arch. The sign (that Mark read) said that the 10 arches closest to the church were also original, and for a long time, there was a big gap between the 10th and 19th arches. Then, in 1989, the arches were rebuilt. We looked at a remaining portion of the 19th arch. It looked really old. I wondered if this mission had 19 arches, since it was the 19th mission.

"Did this mission have 19 arches?" I asked Mishie. "It is the 19th mission."

Before Mishie could answer, Mark butted into our conversation. "No, of course not!"

"Why?" I asked him.

"Just think," he said. "If all of the missions were like that, how many arches would the first mission have?"

"One."

"Exactly."

"So what's wrong with that? It would be cool to see a mission with only one arch."

"No, it wouldn't."

"I think it would. Then people wouldn't have to read signs to figure out what number mission it was. They'd just count the arches."

"You know, I think I'd rather read a sign than count arches. It's faster."

"That's not faster! You could count one arch much faster than read a whole sign."

"What about 19 arches? Or 20? Or 21?"

"I could count to 21 faster than you could read a sign."

"Oh, yeah?"

"Yeah."

"Prove it."

"Okay. Read that sign about the original 19th arch, while I count to 21. We'll see who wins."

Mark said, "Go!" and then I said, "I'm done."

"You can't be done that fast."

"I am. I counted to 21."

"You didn't."

"I did. By 21s."

"Humph!" said Mark, and walked away.

Mishie quietly flew up to me and said, "This mission had 22 arches."

Finally, our outside tour was finished. We came inside to the vestment room. In the vestment room, there were lots of vestments in glass cases designed to look like closets. I saw a gold one, but the Golden Mission wasn't in it. If it was, the vestment would be all lumpy. Mishie said that there was one that had been worn by Father Junipero Serra, but she forgot which one it was.

After going through the model room, which I can't remember very much of, we ended up in the artifact room, with lots of different artifacts important to the mission. In the center of the room, there were some very large books in a glass case. The thing is the books were written in Latin. So, we couldn't understand them. Mark acted disappointed, but, he isn't a very good actor, so I could tell he already knew the books wouldn't be in English.

Next, Mark, Mishie and I visited the Madonna Chapel. It was like a miniature church. Up front, there was a niche that a Madonna stood in. Above the Madonna, was a statue of the crucifixion. It was a little bit scary to me.

After exiting the Madonna chapel, we strode into the church. The walls had a pattern of flowers on them. The flowers went all the way around the church, and sometimes they went over statues in niches. It looked like the flowers were growing on a vine, and it was really pretty. There was also a Rosario (Lady of Rosary) set in a space in the wall. I thought the statue of her was really likable. On the altar, there was a statue of Saint Agnes, the patroness saint of this mission. The unique thing about her was that she was all lit up. A light in front of her was shining, which made her bright. The one thing I didn't like about the church was that there was a statue up front that frightened me. Otherwise, the church was splendid.

After searching on the grounds a tad bit more, Mark, Mishie and I decided it was time to leave.

We stood outside the exit. "Here we go," Mishie said, and we were seeing houses, trees, and roads once again.

Favorite Things at Mission Santa Ines

1. Outside, in the garden, there was a sign that had the **story of Pasquala**, an Indian girl who alerted the priest of Indians coming to destroy the mission. Because of Pasquala's warning, Mission Santa Ines was saved.
2. When we were done touring the rose/cactus garden, we got to see the **original 19th arch**. Only part of it was left, but that didn't make it boring!
3. Mark, Mishie, and I walked under this **arbor** that had some sort of **bean** or something growing on it. They looked a lot like peas, but I don't think peas grow on a vine. They could have been vanilla beans, but I don't know! But, they were awesome, so I guess that's all that really matters!
4. By the garden, there was a very cool **model** of **Mission Santa Ines**. It made the mission look like it was made out of **bricks**. I loved it!
5. On the side entrance to the church, there was a **wavy design on the door**. I liked it, and Mishie told us for about the billionth time what it signifies (the River of Life).

Mission Twenty
Mission San Rafael Arcangel
(Founded: 1817)

San Rafael, CA

* *Mission of Bodily Healing*

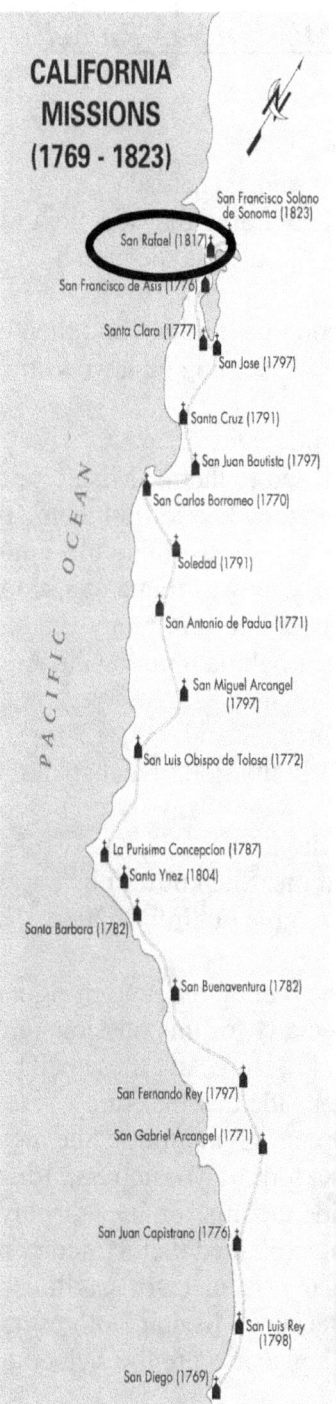

Twentieth Mission: Mission San Rafael

"*W*hoa!" I exclaimed. "That's…"

"Not the mission," Mishie said. "That is."

Mishie pointed to the little building that was next to the gigantic church I had seen. "That building is the parish church."

We hovered above the ground a little bit, and then we landed. Mark noticed the three bells hanging on a wood frame in front of the chapel.

"Those are cool," Mark said. "Did-"

"Yes, special things happened to them," Mishie said. "One time, the bells were lost, and they had to find them. They were found in the strangest places. One was found in a church in El Cajon, a town by San Diego. One was found at a school in Fallon. It had been used as a school bell for many years. The third one had been used as a dinner bell on a big ranch. And the fourth one-"

"Fourth one? I only see three," I said.

"There's a fourth one. It's at the side of a chapel in the center of downtown San Rafael."

"Anything else?" asked Mark.

"Um…" Mishie looked at me. She knows I hate it when Mark takes notes. But she loves to give out information.

"Sure," I said.

"Okay," Mishie said. "The bell on the bottom right and the bell on the top were cast especially for this mission, and the other bell was traded with a whaling ship. And these bells aren't original. The originals are inside the museum."

Then Mishie noticed a docent giving tours. She met up with her, and the docent gave us a tour of Mission San Rafael.

We started our tour outside the mission by a display case with a map in it. The docent explained that Mission San Rafael was originally built to be an asistencia, or satellite, or extension of Mission Dolores. Because Mission Dolores had a massive death rate, they needed a place where the sick could be cured. The weather was warmer in San Rafael, and the people at Mission Dolores thought that might improve the health of the ill ones. After ten years San Rafael became successful enough to be given the position of a full-fledged mission.

They named it "Mission San Rafael" because Saint Raphael was God's healing messenger, and this mission had a lot to do with healing.

The docent wasn't done giving out information yet! She had more to tell us. This meant Mark had more notes to take, which he didn't need to do, but wanted to do for some strange reason.

Mission San Rafael looks different from when it did a while ago. There was an earthquake, and the mission came tumbling down. They were going to rebuild it, but no one knew what the mission looked like.

Years later, Mariano Vallejo made a sketch of what he could remember of the old mission. We viewed that sketch in the museum. There was a rectangular door on the bottom, a square window on top of that, and a triangular window on top of that.

Then a postcard manufacturing company made postcards of the 21 California missions. The postcard man decided that Mission San Rafael looked too plain, so he copied the window from the Carmel mission, and he put that on the mission, instead of the square window. The new window looked fancier and better. Then, instead of the triangle window above that, he copied the window from Carmel again. So there were the same two windows on top of the door, one being slightly smaller than the other. Oh, and speaking of the door, it was no longer rectangular. They made it a dome-like shape.

The docent also said that this was the only mission with *nothing* left from the original mission (excluding the three bells in the museum). It was all a replica.

"What about Mission Santa Cruz?" Mark asked. "They built a replica of it on a different site. Holy Cross Catholic Church was built on the original site of the mission. Doesn't it have nothing left, *too*?"

Mark likes to prove people wrong. And he's very good at it, I must admit. And when he's talking he says it in this smart-aleck voice that's really annoying. Then, when he's done proving you wrong, he'll put his head up like he's oh-so-smart (and he's not). He even does this to adults, which is *really* disrespectful, but that's just the way Mark is.

"Well," said the docent, "Doesn't Mission Santa Cruz still have that little bit of wall behind the new church?"

"Oh, yeah..." Mark said. Then he turned red, and he pulled his hat down over his eyes. He tried to walk with his hat still over his eyes, which he thought we would laugh at. But we didn't laugh at him until he ran into the chapel door. He pushed his hat up after that.

We walked into the chapel, and we were going to tour it, but some schoolchildren were in there, so we decided to come back to it later.

Our next stop was the museum. It was tiny, and it was sharing rooms with the gift shop. I really liked the models of Mission San Rafael that some 4th graders made. One had a roof made from red licorice. Unfortunately, it wasn't edible. You could take the licorice roof off this model, and when you did, you could see inside. There were little beds with little people inside them. This made sense because Mission San Rafael used to be an active hospital. It was really neat. There was also a gigantic painting of Saint Raphael, the patron saint of this mission. Mark pointed out that he had wings. I don't think I recall any of the other patron saints having wings.

Since we didn't get to tour the chapel thoroughly, we went back inside it. I noticed the flags hanging from the walls. They represented governments that the mission had once been ruled under. I also noticed the Stations of the Cross were really pretty. They were like gold sculptures. Too bad they weren't Golden Mission sculptures.

"Wow, Mishie," I said. "These are really beautiful. How come they're...like that?"

"Well, there used to be just regular wooden Stations of the Cross in the chapel. Then, there was an opportunity to buy new ones in 1949. They looked better and were prettier. So they bought them, and that was that."

I looked at the altar. It was pretty also, and it was all gold. I noticed that the altar sort of matched the Stations of the Cross. In the center niche was a statue of Saint Raphael. To the left was a statue or Our Lady of Guadalupe, and to the right was a statue of Saint Joseph. Saint Joseph and Our Lady of Guadalupe both had freshly cut flowers near them.

We exited the church, and then we stood outside the mission. We were going to go inside the big parish church to see if we could find the Golden Mission. I thought it would be open since it was right next to the mission. But Mark disagreed.

"Why wouldn't it be?" I asked him.

"Because," he said, "It's not *really* part of Mission San Rafael, is it? I mean, it's not listed on the map."

"So? It's probably still open."

"I don't think so. If it were just a regular parish church that wasn't next to a mission, they wouldn't leave the doors open. Some burglar could break in at any moment. That wouldn't be logical."

"Not everything is logical like you think it is, Mark."

"Things *should* be logical. *You* should be logical."

"I'm logical! You're just too dumb to know it."

"I'm not dumb!"

"Yes, you are."

"Would you like me to prove that I'm not dumb? When we get home, I'll pull out my report card and show you."

"Uh…" I really didn't want Mark showing me all of his boring report cards, so I said, "That's okay. I don't need to know anymore. Let's just see if the church is open."

But it was closed. Mark, Mishie and I decided to leave.

"1, 2, 3!" Mishie said, and we left Mission San Rafael.

On our way to the next mission, I spotted a Subway. "I'm sort of hungry; let's eat."

"What restaurant do you see?" Mark asked. "Is it a Quizno's?"

"No, it's a Subway. Will that work for you?"

He sighed. "Whatever."

We had a quick lunch, Mark wiped his hands with a napkin finger by finger, and then we continued flying to the next mission.

Favorite Things at Mission San Rafael

1. In the museum, there were **models** of **Mission San Rafael** that 4th graders had donated to the mission. My favorite model was one with red **licorice** for a **roof**.
2. **Outside** the mission, there were **three bells** that had an interesting story.
3. In the chapel, there are beautiful **Stations of the Cross**. At first, they didn't have Stations this pretty, but in 1949, there was an opportunity to buy new ones. They bought them, and now they have Stations that are newer and prettier.

4. We started our tour with the docent outside, by a **map**. The map was really unique because it didn't just show the mission as it was today, but as it was when it was still an active mission. Light lines showed where mission used to be, and dark lines showed where mission is now. I noticed that the mission today is mostly a school! I also noticed that a quadrangle was never built at the mission. Mishie said this was because they didn't mean to make it an actual mission, so they didn't build a quadrangle, and never did.

Mission Twenty-One

Mission San Francisco Solano

(Founded: 1823)

Sonoma, CA

Sonoma Mission

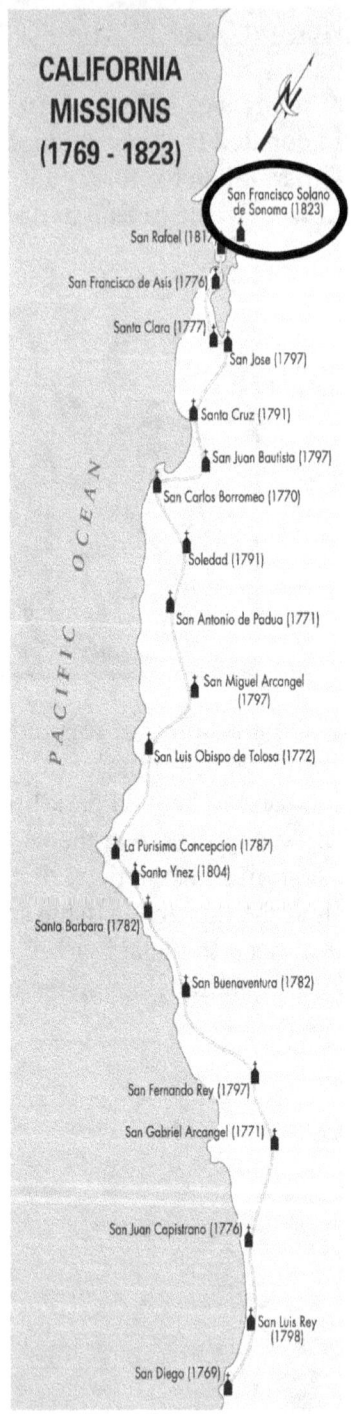

Twenty-First Mission: Mission San Francisco Solano

Since we didn't find the Golden Mission at any of the other missions we've been to, I was really confident that it would be at this one. As soon as we landed, I started running around the outside garden like I had too much sugar or I just got off a fun roller coaster or something like that.

I couldn't wait to find it. The Golden Mission was here! I couldn't wait to hold it and see it and touch it and smell it...if it had a smell.

It was very clever to hide the Golden Mission at the last mission. I mean, it's just so obvious! First, you would look at all the other missions, not find it, and then, at the last one, you would! The last place you think of looking is *always* where something will be...most of the time.

Why didn't I think of looking at the last mission first? I knew it would be here. Well, I guess I would miss out on all the fun if I only visited this one and not the others. No matter, it was a great experience touring the other missions.

I thought that I should get back to looking and stop daydreaming. So I started looking around like mad again.

I was too busy looking around like a crazy person, I didn't even notice the El Camino Real bell and plaque right in front of my face. Once Mark read it, he told me that this was where the historic route ended. I was sort of confused because I thought the road ended in San Francisco by Mission Dolores. But then Mishie reminded me that was how Father Serra knew it, but they extended it after his death so it could reach two newly built missions: Mission San Rafael and Mission San Francisco Solano (Sonoma).

After hanging out a little more around the El Camino Real bell, we toured the garden. There were lots of poppies growing there, and they reminded me of the Wicked Witch of the West from "The Wizard of Oz." I love that movie.

Another plant I liked was the cactus plant. But I will understand if you want to call it a prickly pear plant, because it was covered in prickly pear! You could hardly see any of the cacti. Just prickly pear. I looked inside it, but all I could see was prickly pear. It didn't really matter, though, because I knew the Golden Mission wasn't in there anyway. If it was, the cactus plant would be glowing or something.

When we finished with our careful examining of the plants, (I went crazy and looked inside them, under them, etc.) I decided I wanted to go inside the museum. But Brainiac Mark just *had* to read the State Historic Landmark sign. I didn't really read it, but when I got to the bottom of the sign I saw that it was State Historic Landmark #3! I've been to a place that was, like, Landmark #700!

Anyway, I eventually got my way and (after Mishie said, "Mishie service,") we went into the museum. In the first room, there was this model-like thingy that looked neat. There were also three bells on display. The Golden Mission was not under any of the bells. Since they were too heavy to lift, and I probably wasn't allowed to touch them anyway, I had Mishie levitate them with her powers. My favorite items in there were the pieces of adobe or stone or rock or something that had a big cat's paw prints in it. The big cat could have been a cougar, mountain lion, jaguar, panther, tiger, lion…I don't know!

I thought the next room was super! There were paintings of all the missions displayed everywhere on the walls. Virgil Jorgensen, the man who painted them, was a really good artist! These paintings were of the missions before they were restored, and they were in pretty bad shape! I looked at one of Mission Soledad, and it was mostly just a few rotting adobe bricks. I looked at all of the paintings, but there wasn't a painting of the Golden Mission. If there was, I would grab it off the shelf, stuff it in my bag, and quickly take it home with me!

In room number three, there were a bunch of signs telling about stuff that had to do with the missions. I remember a sign about the Indians, and one about El Camino Real. I didn't even bother looking here, because the Golden Mission couldn't be on a sign or anything.

Next, Mark, Mishie and I visited the chapel. I asked why there were only painted columns on the altar.

"This mission had a short life," Mishie stated. "It was founded in 1823, and I think it only lived 11 years."

Mark did some quick math in his head, one of his abnormal skills, and said, "So it started to crumble, or the Indians left or whatever in…1834?"

"Yep. You figured that out quick. You're pretty good at math, Mark," said Mishie.

I hate it when people compliment Mark and ignore me, so I interrupted. "You didn't answer my question. I asked why their columns were painted, not how long the mission lived."

Mishie glared at me. She has this problem with getting to the point and not giving all this other not-needed factual information. "I was getting to that." Mishie gave me another not-needed dirty look, and then went on with why the columns were painted.

"As I said before, *this mission only lived for 11 years*, and since it had a short life, there wasn't much time to trade tallow and hides, and all that. They didn't have enough money to get real columns or other decorations, so they had it painted. Look at those swags of material painted on the wall, over there."

"Over where?"

"Above the pulpit."

"What's a pulpit?"

"The thingy that the priest stands in to give his sermon."

"Oh…" I said, slightly embarrassed.

"Anyway, the swags of material there are painted, just like the columns on the altar. If this mission had lived longer, like Mission San Diego or Mission San Carlos, then there wouldn't be painted swags, there would be real swags."

When Mishie finished her 10-hour speech, I started to look around. I looked at the not-that-scary Stations of the

Cross, and for the first time, I noticed a horse in Station Number 10. There might have also been one in Station Number 8, but I'm not completely sure. The horse could be something unique to this mission, or I could have just been not looking hard enough, and the horse was in every mission.

Also, there were no chairs or pews. This was because when the Indians came to mass, they sat on the floor. This mission is also a State Historic Park, and no people come to mass anymore.

I noticed that some light was pouring in from a window. It made a big square of light on the tile floor. I thought it would be the perfect place for the Golden Mission to be, since it was in the light. And then I saw the Golden Mission in the light! It was just as I imagined it, all gold and beautiful. I ran up to it shouting and yelling and jumping all at the same time. When I got there, I got really disappointed. It was a drawing of Mission San Francisco Solano colored gold. It was propped up by a popsicle stick. Mark jumped out from behind the pulpit and said, "Surprise!"

"Ha, ha," I said sarcastically. "That was so funny."

"I know!" Mark said, putting the drawing back in his backpack. "You looked so crazy running around like you found it! It was hilarious!"

I sighed at him and forgot about it.

After searching in the chapel a little more, we went out into the courtyard. When I got outside, the first thing I noticed was the windows. The walls were really thick, and the windows were set really deep inside them.

Another thing I liked about the courtyard was the fountain. It had a very unique design. The water flowed out of the fountain, and into a ditch dug around it. The Golden Mission wasn't inside the fountain, and fish weren't either. But there was money. Lots and lots of coins. It was pretty cool.

Then, we went into an area in the back. There was a big, white beehive oven (that the Golden Mission could have been in, but wasn't), and a bell (I couldn't resist ringing it). The bell was really high up; I had to stand on my tippy-toes to reach it. I also liked the roof at this place. It looked like it was made out of twigs and sticks. It reminded me of the roof at Mission Santa Cruz.

We walked around and searched a little more, and finally left that part of the mission. There are two parts. The part we were going to next contained another museum, a movie theatre, and another gift shop. I knew the Golden Mission would be there!

First, we hurried into the soldiers' barracks. There were lots of beds, and a table with plates, cups, bowls, and playing cards on it. Apparently, the soldiers played card games. There were also these really big and pointy weapons by the side of the beds. I thought that was a good place to keep them because then no one would steal them! When I find the Golden Mission here, I will keep it right by my bed so Mark wouldn't come into my room and steal it. I will put an alarm around it too, so even if he tried to touch it, I would know. But unfortunately, I didn't find it here.

Shortly after, we went into the other museum. It had a saddle in a glass case, and there was some of the material used to build the mission in a glass case also. But the Golden Mission wasn't in any of the glass cases.

The movie Mark, Mishie, and I saw after that was about the history of the mission. It was sort of boring because it wasn't about the history of the *Golden* Mission. (He, he!) It said that this was the only mission that had been constructed under Mexican authority. It talked about the Indians, the founder, and Mariano Vallejo.

Father Altimira, a priest who wanted his own mission, got the California governor's permission to build a mission, but not the church's. He went ahead and started building the mission. But the church was furious with him and made him stop building. Eventually, the church gave him permission to finish San Francisco Solano.

On our way back to the mission to see the Indian memorial, there was this little 4, 5, or 6-year-old kid running around. I started laughing because while he was running, he was shouting out something really funny: "I'm feeling the sun! I'm feeling the sun! I'm feeling the sun! I'm feeling the sun!"

He kept shouting this over and over and it eventually got annoying, but it was still very amusing. It got stuck in my head, though, and to get it out, I said, "I'm feeling the gold! I'm feeling the gold! I'm feeling the gold! I'm feeling the gold!" because I could just feel I was really close to finding the Golden Mission.

We walked a bit, and then we got to the Indian memorial. It was a gigantic block made out of granite (probably). Too bad it wasn't made out of gold. It had a bunch of Indian names on it, like Barbata, Secunda, Joseea, Romana, Gertandi, and Zenobio! I liked their names because I had never heard of people with such original names until now!

"So there's more to the mission, right?" I asked Mishie. We hadn't found the Golden Mission, so I was assuming that there was more. I mean, it *had* to be at this mission. It wasn't at any of the others! There was no way it couldn't be here!

Mark stared at me with the do-you-see-any-more-of-this-mission-anywhere-when-you-do-call-me-my-cell-phone-number-is-1-866-IMA-LUSR look. I stared at him with the I-want-to-stick-my-tongue-out-at-you look.

"Well..." Mishie wasn't looking at us. She was looking at the ground. I figured that wasn't a good sign. "We're done with this one. Sorry, Allison."

I wanted to scream, *"What?!"* but I couldn't. That would be rude. My mouth dropped open. And it was still open when Mishie pulled us off the ground and had us on our way back to Riverside. I left Mission San Francisco Solano disappointed, and slightly confused. How could we not find the Golden Mission? It seemed impossible. How could we not find it?

Favorite Things at Mission San Francisco Solano

1. In front of the mission, there was this **cactus** plant with **prickly pear** all over it. You could hardly see any of the cacti; it was *all* prickly pears.
2. In the **courtyard**, there was a **fountain** with a really neat design. It overflowed, and then the water fell into a ditch dug around the fountain. I really enjoyed it.
3. Outside, in the **courtyard**, there was a **bell** that I rang. I liked the sound, and I had to stand on my tippy-toes to reach it because it was pretty high up. It was super neat!
4. In the museum, there was a block of stone or adobe or something that had a big **cat's paw print** in it. I really liked looking at it.
5. In front of the mission, there were lots of **poppies**! They were pretty, and reminded me of a scene from the Wizard of Oz.
6. Inside the museum, there were **watercolor paintings** of the 21 California **missions**. What I liked about them was that they didn't look like they did today. These paintings weren't of restored missions, but of falling-apart missions!
7. In **Station of the Cross X,** there was a **horse**. I liked this because I have never seen this before, and it was unusual.
8. Inside the church, there were **painted columns** on the altar, and **painted swags** of material above the pulpit. Since this mission only lived for 11 years, they weren't rich enough to get real swags or real columns. I thought this story was interesting.

The Golden Mission Discovered All over California

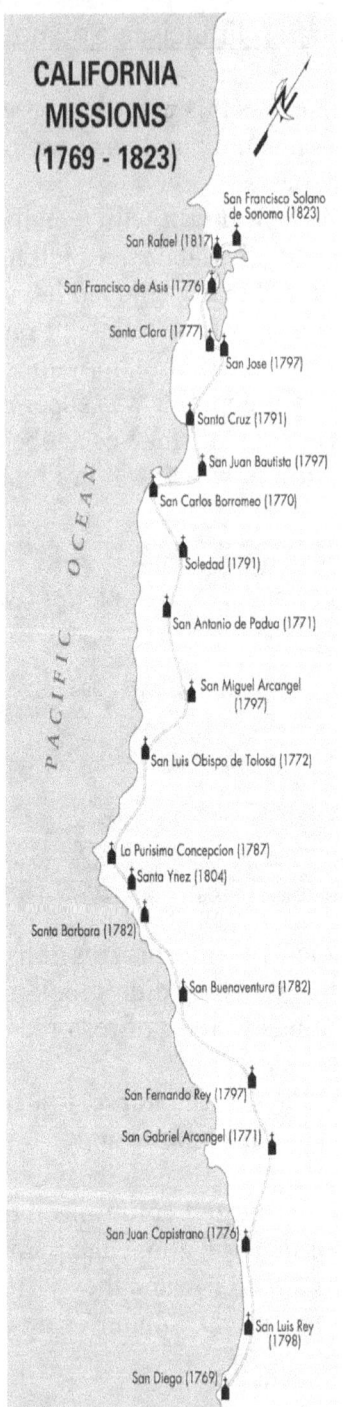

The Golden Mission Discovered

I was beginning to think this was all for nothing. Mark and I were really discouraged. This was the first time I actually *failed* on a mystery. Or in this case, a mission. Mark looked a little happier because he's failed before, and knows how to deal with it.

I couldn't believe it though. How could we not find it? We looked in every single possible place. Every mission. Every nook and cranny. Every hole in the ground, behind every gate. In every building. Every …

"Allison?" Mishie asked. She stared at me with her big, happy eyes. Too big. Too happy. How could she be happy in a time like this? We had failed! How could Mishie be happy when we had failed? How dare she! How dare Mishie be happy! No one in their right mind would be happy right now! No one …

"Allison?" Mishie repeated a little louder. "Are you okay?"

"Yeah," I lied, then sniffed and wiped my eyes.

"Crybaby," Mark muttered under his breath.

I wanted to yell at him. Scream at him. Punch him in his freaky noodlehead face. He would be crying if he failed for the first time, too. But I controlled it. I ignored him, instead of getting into an argument, and I calmed down.

Mishie whispered something to Mark that I was pretty sure I wasn't supposed to hear. I knew we weren't anywhere near home yet when I heard Mishie tell us to land. I landed, and when I did, I saw that I was right by CDA headquarters in Hollywood.

"This it?" Mishie asked Mark.

"That's the one," Mark said pointing to the structure with big white neon letters: NBC. The CDA headquarters was disguised as a NBC building. This was so no one knew about CDA except the members.

We led Mishie to the food court. I ordered a Hawaiian pizza with extra pineapple, extra ham, and some pepperoni just for fun, and Mark ordered boring cheese.

At our private table, I plopped onto the seat, looked downward and sighed dramatically. I was hoping Mishie would notice me, and tell me why we didn't find the Golden Mission. But Mishie didn't notice me, because she was too busy whispering with Mark behind my back. I wondered what they were plotting.

I sighed an immensely loud sigh, and Mishie still didn't notice me. Then, I sighed an *immensely, immensely, extremely, extremely* loud sigh, and I blew all the napkins off the table.

"What?" asked Mark in the I'm-annoyed-Allison-stop-it-it's-not-like-I-do-this-to-you-wait-I-do-it-all-the-time voice.

"I want to talk to Mishie," I said.

"She's busy," said Mark, "getting our pizzas."

"Oh..." I said, looking up for the first time and realizing Mishie wasn't there.

I decided to wait, and think up what I would say to Mishie when she came back. Nah, that was boring. I'd just pout, because there was nothing better to do.

How come we didn't find it? How could we? We looked everywhere. Everywhere! And we visited 21 missions. Were there more than 21, and we just didn't visit them all? No. Mishie's the mission expert, and if she says there are only 21 missions, then she has to be correct. Could the question have a different meaning? The Golden Mission. It had a nice ring to it. Maybe the news anchorman wasn't talking about a little model of a mission made out of gold. No, not at all. He might've been talking about which mission was the best. But, I couldn't think which one was the best, or which one was the worst. They were all special in their own kind of way. They were all special in their own kind of way. All special in their own kind of way. All special... All special...

I sat up really straight. That was it.

When Mishie came back I ate my Hawaiian pizza with extra pineapple, extra ham, and some pepperoni just for fun very slowly and quietly. I heard Mark whisper to Mishie, "I think my sister's planning something. She's usually not this silent."

When Mark wasn't done, and I was, I asked Mishie the question I had been planning while I ate lunch.

"Mishie?" Mishie directed her large brown eyes toward me.

"Yes?"

"I was just wondering . . . how come we didn't find the Golden Mission? Was it all just a trick? Did we skip a mission?" And then I remembered what I was thinking about while waiting for the pizza, and *my* eyes got big.

"Mishie," I said slowly, "I got it. There was no Golden Mission. That's why we never found it. It wasn't an object. It was the missions themselves. They were gold! They were all special in their own kind of way, Mishie." I said Mishie's name even though I wasn't talking to her anymore. I was talking to myself. Saying my thoughts out loud. I knew now, I knew what the Golden Mission was. All of them!

"All of them." I kept talking. "They were all gold. They were all special. Not one, all. I get it, Mishie. I get it! I figured it out!"

Mishie smiled at me. "Yeah," she said. "But I think you owe Mark an apology. He was right all along. By reading the signs, he gathered useful information about the missions, which probably made them more enjoyable. *That* was also the gold."

I sighed. I don't like apologizing very much, because it's sort of like admitting you're wrong, which I hate to do in front of Mark. He gets all boastful and bratty afterward because he thinks he's smarter than you. But I did it anyway.

"I'm sorry I never listened to you," I said. "You were right the whole time and I never gave you a chance. You just wanted to take your time and *really* search for the Golden Mission. I wanted to hurry and get it done. Well, I'm sorry, and next time I'll be more understanding."

Mark smiled. For a moment I thought he was going to say something like, "This is the day you finally realized that I am always right." Or "Wow, you finally figured out which one of us is *really* the dumb one." But he didn't say either of these things. Actually, what he said was *funny*. To both of us.

"Okay," he said. "Let me just get revenge on you. There's something I want to say…you're a noodlehead of a sister."

Then we both doubled up laughing because being called a noodlehead isn't really insulting, and it's something I call him *a lot*. I then realized I wasn't that unlucky to have a brother like him. Actually, I think I'm pretty fortunate.

Mishie didn't want to interrupt, so she waited a while before she said, "Sorry about the whispering. I thought taking you to the CDA headquarters would be a good idea, but that didn't seem to work, so Mark and I were thinking of what to do next. But now it looks like you're okay, so we don't have to worry. You know, you were kind of *down*, so we had to figure out where to take you to cheer you *up*."

I laughed at her down and up joke just to be polite, because it wasn't very good. It was pitiful. Mishie needed joke lessons just as bad as Mark. In a few minutes, Mark, Mishie and I had left the food court. We flew the rest of the way back to Riverside, where we parted.

When we got to our house, Mishie said, "You know, I'm not just a mission tour guide. I can help you with your next mystery, too."

"Thanks," Mark and I said in unison, and we ran inside the house, wondering what our next *mission* would be.

I found special things at every mission. That's why they were all gold. And remember, my favorite things make a great "I Spy" game when you tour the missions. Also, I hope you find your own gold on your fantastic mission adventure.

Mission San Juan Capistrano

San Juan Capistrano, CA

Saint Joseph's Day

Saint Joseph's Day
Mission San Juan Capistrano

*O*ne day, while Mark and I were doing homework, Mishie rang our doorbell and said that there was a special yearly event going on at Mission San Juan Capistrano. It was today, on St. Joseph's Day, celebrating the swallows' return to the mission. She asked if Mark and I would like to come. We said yes, and Mishie flew us to the celebration.

First, a nice lady named Mechelle Lawrence came onstage and gave a not-too-boring, five-minute speech. Then, Renee Bondi sang the song, "When the Swallows Come Back to Capistrano," by Leon Rene. (Hey! We heard about that before! Remember the room with the electric fan?)

After that, some eighth-graders were introduced wearing period costumes such as princesses, princes, kings, and queens. They were recognized for good behavior and their grades. Something Mark would get, I bet. Shortly after, kindergarteners dressed up as miniature monks sang a song, first-graders dressed up as swallows danced, and I found the fourth-graders quite entertaining…they dressed up as old people, and danced with fake canes. The rest of the school – 2nd, 3rd, 5th, 6th, 7th, and 8th graders – had dresses and outfits sort of like tuxedos on. They danced to Mexican music.

The Tushmal Singers are a group of women who are descended from the Indians who built the mission. They sang neat Indian songs that I really enjoyed.

Next was Mission Docent Society Trivia Game Show. Long name. It's also called, "Are You Smarter than a California 4th Grader?" Mishie told us all the answers, so we got a couple prizes. But, we didn't answer all the questions because that would have been unfair to the other people who didn't have Mishie.

Kathryn Fitzmaurice, an author, presented a Readers' Theater from her book "The Year the Swallows Came Early." I bought one of her books and had her sign it. It was really exciting!

Then Mark and I exited the stage and we went over to the front of the mission to hear the bells ring. While Mishie got quesadillas from Pedro's Tacos across the street (that place has *great* food!). Mark and I listened to Renee Bondi sing again. Then Mishie came back, and we did the Mission Docent Society Trivia Game Show again.

Jacque Nunez, who was a descendant from the Indians who built this mission, talked about the Indian culture. She played music, showed dances–with the help of her son and very cute granddaughter–and she let some children play with the rattles and other instruments the Indians used.

Since the fashion show they were supposed to have was canceled, our day there was done. Mishie flew us home and we continued to do our homework. I told Mishie that she could have just left me at the mission, because I hated doing homework. She laughed at me and said I was very funny, even though that wasn't supposed to be a joke.

Go to this celebration at Mission San Juan Capistrano! You won't be disappointed!

Favorite Things at Saint Joseph's Day Celebration

1. **Children** from Mission Parish School appeared as **princesses, princes, monks, swallows, old men, and women,** and they wore **fancy dresses.** I really enjoyed their performances.
2. The Mission Docent Society **Trivia Game** Show was super fun. I liked the prizes.
3. An **author**, Kathryn Fitzmaurice, came and **read** a little out of her book. I thought it was really interesting, and I liked it quite a bit.
4. When Jacque Nunez talked about the **Indian** culture, she had her adorable **granddaughter** come up. Unfortunately, she started crying onstage, and she had to dance her special dance in Mommy's arms. (She eventually calmed down, though.)
5. Mark, Mishie, and I re–visited the Great Stone Church. This time, we noticed the awesome **shells** and neat-looking **rocks embedded in the walls**. There was this one shiny, smooth, black rock that I liked a lot.

Appendix

CALIFORNIA MISSIONS (1769 - 1823)

- San Francisco Solano de Sonoma (1823)
- San Rafael (1817)
- San Francisco de Asis (1776)
- Santa Clara (1777)
- San Jose (1797)
- Santa Cruz (1791)
- San Juan Bautista (1797)
- San Carlos Borromeo (1770)
- Soledad (1791)
- San Antonio de Padua (1771)
- San Miguel Arcangel (1797)
- San Luis Obispo de Tolosa (1772)
- La Purisima Concepcion (1787)
- Santa Ynez (1804)
- Santa Barbara (1782)
- San Buenaventura (1782)
- San Fernando Rey (1797)
- San Gabriel Arcangel (1771)
- San Juan Capistrano (1776)
- San Luis Rey (1798)
- San Diego (1769)

CALIFORNIA MISSIONS (1769 - 1823)

- San Francisco Solano de Sonoma (1823)
- San Rafael (1817)
- San Francisco de Asis (1776)
- Santa Clara (1777)
- San Jose (1797)
- Santa Cruz (1791)
- San Juan Bautista (1797)
- San Carlos Borromeo (1770)
- Soledad (1791)
- San Antonio de Padua (1771)
- San Miguel Arcangel (1797)
- San Luis Obispo de Tolosa (1772)
- La Purisima Concepcion (1787)
- Santa Ynez (1804)
- Santa Barbara (1782)
- San Buenaventura (1782)
- San Fernando Rey (1797)
- San Gabriel Arcangel (1771)
- San Juan Capistrano (1776)
- San Luis Rey (1798)
- San Diego (1769)

Basilicas

San Francisco, Carmel, San Juan Capistrano, San Diego, CA

Basilicas

*F*irst of all, what *are* basilicas? A basilica is a certain kind of church. It meets the standards a church needs to meet in order to be a basilica. Once a basilica, a church gets various privileges.

Four of the missions have basilica churches. These missions are, **Mission San Diego, Mission San Carlos Borromeo** (Carmel)**, Mission San Francisco** (Mission Dolores), and **Mission San Juan Capistrano** (Mission Basilica San Juan Capistrano).

The word 'basilica' comes from a Latin word describing a Roman public structure that was usually positioned in a Roman town. In Hellenistic cities, public basilicas appeared in 2nd century B.C.!

How can you identify a basilica? Well, a basilica church always had a conopaeum, which is an item that looked like an umbrella, or canopy. It is yellow and red. The conopaeum can also be called a papilio, sinicchio, ombrellino, or umbraculum.

In conclusion, basilicas are just a specific type of church. Four of the missions have basilica churches. You know a church is a basilica by its conopaeum. Basilicas are great!

El Camino Real Throughout California

*The Royal Road

CALIFORNIA MISSIONS (1769 - 1823)

- San Francisco Solano de Sonoma (1823)
- San Rafael (1817)
- San Francisco de Asis (1776)
- Santa Clara (1777)
- San Jose (1797)
- Santa Cruz (1791)
- San Juan Bautista (1797)
- San Carlos Borromeo (1770)
- Soledad (1791)
- San Antonio de Padua (1771)
- San Miguel Arcangel (1797)
- San Luis Obispo de Tolosa (1772)
- La Purisima Concepcion (1787)
- Santa Ynez (1804)
- Santa Barbara (1782)
- San Buenaventura (1782)
- San Fernando Rey (1797)
- San Gabriel Arcangel (1771)
- San Juan Capistrano (1776)
- San Luis Rey (1798)
- San Diego (1769)

El Camino Real

What is El Camino Real? El Camino Real is the road connecting the 21 California missions. It is about **600** miles long, and goes from Mission San Diego de Alcala in San Diego to Mission San Francisco de Asis in San Francisco. (Some say it actually ends in Sonoma.) It was one of the first California state highways.

Translated into English, El Camino Real means: "The Royal Road." It is also sometimes called "The Royal Highway" or "The King's Highway."

Mistakes have been made when people have tried to say, "El Camino Real." Some people refer to it as "The El Camino," which actually translates to "The The Road." Sounds funny, doesn't it? Another often-made mistake is assuming that Camino means Royal and Real means Road. But, it is exactly the opposite. The Spanish language is different from the English language. For instance, instead of one saying 'purple hat', you would say 'hat purple'.

How do you know you're on El Camino Real? Well, every now and then bells are seen alongside the road. These mean you are traveling on El Camino Real. The bells are metal, and have a greenish color. They are about 1 to 2 miles apart. We saw most of them when we were traveling north of San Miguel on Highway 101.

Some people question where El Camino Real actually ends. Since San Francisco Solano is the last mission, and the mission the furthest up north, some people assume the road ends there. Other people think that El Camino Real ends in San Francisco. Well, at first, El Camino Real ended at Mission Dolores in San Francisco. This is how Father Serra knew El Camino Real. In the early 1800's, which was after Father Serra's demise, they decided to extend the road farther up north to reach two more missions, San Rafael and Sonoma. Basically, the original El Camino Real ends in San Francisco. It was extended to establish the other missions later in history.

An unpaved segment of the original road still remains next to Mission San Juan Bautista in San Juan Bautista, CA. When I visited that mission, we walked along the original El Camino Real, and that was really fun.

We took pictures of me at various El Camino Real bells at various missions. At some of the missions, we didn't see the bells, but this doesn't mean they weren't there. At some missions, we weren't really looking for them. I'm pretty sure some of the missions *don't* have an El Camino Real bell in front, but it would probably be fun for you to look and see if all of them do. We didn't notice the El Camino Real bells at: San Carlos (Carmel), San Gabriel, San Francisco, San Juan Capistrano, La Purisima (Lompoc), and Santa Cruz.

As you can see, The Royal Road plays an important part in California mission history. Without this highway, the journeys to the missions would be longer, and more boring. Give thanks to El Camino Real!

CALIFORNIA MISSIONS (1769 - 1823)

- San Francisco Solano de Sonoma (1823)
- San Rafael (1817)
- San Francisco de Asis (1776)
- Santa Clara (1777)
- San Jose (1797)
- Santa Cruz (1791)
- San Juan Bautista (1797)
- San Carlos Borromeo (1770)
- Soledad (1791)
- San Antonio de Padua (1771)
- San Miguel Arcangel (1797)
- San Luis Obispo de Tolosa (1772)
- La Purisima Concepcion (1787)
- Santa Ynez (1804)
- Santa Barbara (1782)
- San Buenaventura (1782)
- San Fernando Rey (1797)
- San Gabriel Arcangel (1771)
- San Juan Capistrano (1776)
- San Luis Rey (1798)
- San Diego (1769)

Father Junipero Serra

Father Junipero Serra

*W*ho was Junipero Serra? Father Serra founded the first nine missions, and was made the padre-president of the Baja California Franciscan missionaries in 1767. He preferred to walk along the coast of California in search of mission sites, but he sometimes rode animals. Bonus fact: *Junipero* means *Juniper* in English.

Serra's full name was Jose Miguel Serra. He was born on November 24, 1713, on the Island of Majorca in Spain. When he was 16, he joined the Order of Friars Minor (also know as: O. F. M.)

Father Serra founded the first nine missions: San Diego, San Carlos, San Antonio, San Gabriel, San Luis Obispo, San Francisco, San Juan Capistrano, Santa Clara, and San Buenaventura. He was working on founding the tenth, Mission Santa Barbara, but he died in the process.

Some of Father Serra's preaching methods were quite different. Sometimes, he would hit his chest extremely hard with a rock or iron crucifix. Or, he would burn his palm with a candle.

Since Mission San Carlos, (Carmel), was believed to be Father Serra's favorite mission, that's where he is buried. It was also the mission where he died. He died on August 28, 1784, and he was 70 years old.

In conclusion, Father Serra was a very important person. He became a Franciscan novice at 16. He was the founder of missions 1-9 and will always be a remembered priest.

Stations of the Cross

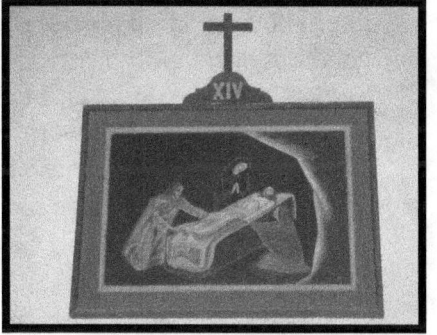

Stations of the Cross

*W*hat are the Stations of the Cross? Well, they are pictures that tell the story, or Passion, of Jesus. The Fourteen Stations of the Cross are also known as The Way of the Cross, Via Dolorosa, Way of Sorrows, or maybe just, The Way. Some people pray to them. This is usually done on Good Friday.

At different times, there were different numbers of Stations of the Cross. They varied from the Seven Stations of the Cross to the Twelve Stations of the Cross and over that.

A Fifteenth Station has been added, "Jesus rises from the dead." This is a recent addition, so I didn't see it at any of the missions. It is optional.

I found unique Stations of the Cross at pretty much every mission. These are the ones that caught my eye in particular. At **Mission San Diego**, they had a set of tile mosaic Stations near the Pieta Garden. At **Mission Santa Clara**, the Stations of the Cross were like colorful sculptures, and there were also words underneath them. At **Mission Santa Cruz**, there were words. There was a wooden carving of a cross, and words underneath the wooden cross that described the Station. At **Mission San Juan Bautista**, they had Stations of the Cross that were on either side of numerous arches in the garden area. At **Mission San Rafael**, the Stations were gold and sculpture-like. They used to have old regular ones but then there was a good opportunity to buy new ones, so they bought them. In Station X at **Mission San Francisco Solano**, there was a horse.

I really liked the written Stations of the Cross at Mission Santa Cruz because they weren't scary to me. At most of the missions, they have bloody paintings of Jesus being crucified and stuff. I don't care for those Stations of the Cross too much.

These are what the Stations say:

I.	Jesus is condemned to death
II.	Jesus carries his cross
III.	Jesus falls the first time
IV.	Jesus meets his blessed Mother.
V.	Simon of Cyrene helps Jesus to carry his cross
VI.	Veronica wipes the face of Jesus
VII.	Jesus falls the second time
VIII.	Jesus speaks to the women of Jerusalem
IX.	Jesus falls the third time
X.	Jesus is stripped of his garments
XI.	Jesus is nailed to the cross
XII.	Jesus dies on the cross
XIII.	Jesus is taken down from the cross
XIV.	Jesus is laid in the sepulcher

To sum it all up, the 14 Stations of the Cross tell the story (Passion) of Jesus. It can be called many different names. A Fifteenth Station has been added, but we don't see it often. Every mission has unique Stations of the Cross. I especially like the ones at Mission Santa Cruz.

Santa Cruz

Santa Clara

Planning a Trip?

Planning a Trip?

*W*hile visiting the missions, we did some other really neat stuff. If you are planning a trip around various missions, you might want to consider taking the time to visit these other fun places. First, I list how much time we spent at each mission and then how much time I think you should allow to visit that particular mission. Also, there are suggestions on where to play, dine, or just have fun!

Since we live in Southern California, most of the trips are from a Southern California starting point. Hope you find this information useful!

Mission San Fernando Rey de Espana
San Fernando, California
We spent 3 hours – Allow 2 to 4 hours
You could probably spend most of the day at this mission, but you could still tour it thoroughly and tour another mission (San Gabriel or San Buenaventura) on the same day if you want. As soon as we left this mission, we went to Mission San Gabriel, so we didn't really do anything around there.

Mission San Gabriel Arcangel
San Gabriel, California
We spent 2½ hours – Allow 2 to 3 hours
We did this mission on the same day we did Mission San Fernando. But, if you're going to do San Gabriel and San Fernando on the same day, make sure you start early, because you could end late and you don't want to be rushed.

Mission San Juan Capistrano
San Juan Capistrano, California
We spent 7 hours – Allow 4 to 8 hours

It could take you a whole day to tour this mission! Make sure you plan on spending lots of time there. There is also a really good Mexican food place across the street called, "Pedro's Tacos." Since the Old Stone Church is in ruins, they built a new church in back of the mission. Make sure you see that too.

Mission San Luis Rey
Oceanside, California
We spent 2½ hours – Allow 1 to 2½ hours

This is a mission that won't take very long. It is more of a retreat, and not much of it is open to the public. You could probably tour this mission on the same day as you tour Mission San Diego, or *maybe* Mission San Juan Capistrano. (But probably not. San Juan Capistrano is a large mission). On the day we were there, the lavanderia was locked up. Make sure to ask them to open it up for you. It is worth seeing.

Mission San Diego de Alcala
San Diego, California
We spent 3½ hours – Allow 2 to 4 hours

If the archeologists let you dig with them, then you will definitely stay longer, depending on how long they let you dig. An interesting train station (if you like trains, like my brother) and Balboa Park (lots of great museums) are near, so you might want to go to those places, too.

Cambria / Santa Barbara Trip

*W*e stayed in Cambria for a few days. It was close to 4 missions, and allowed us to do other fun things. While in Cambria we played on Moonstone Beach and collected rare moonstones (but they weren't really that hard to find). We also visited the elephant seals at Piedras Blancas (8 miles north of San Simeon) and visited Hearst Castle (in San Simeon), a very awesome castle. You need to go there.

Mission San Buenaventura
Ventura, California
We spent 2½ hours – Allow 1½ to 3 hours

This mission could be toured with another mission (San Fernando or Santa Barbara), even though we didn't do that. We stopped at this mission on our drive up to Cambria. There is a wonderful fountain across the street, and there is a small fire truck museum (which is viewed only from the outside) by the fountain. Before leaving Ventura, we ate at a pizza place (Ferraro's Italian Restaurant) with really good cheese pizza.

Mission San Luis Obispo de Tolosa
San Luis Obispo, California
We spent 2 hours – Allow 1½ to 2½ hours

When we visited the mission, the church was closed due to restoration. If it is open when you visit you should allow more time. This mission could also be toured with another mission. Some nights, they have a Farmer's Market in downtown San Luis Obispo. We caught it the night before touring the mission. It was really neat, and we ate vanilla filled churros. We also went to Bubblegum Alley (next to 733 Higuera Street), an alley with bubble gum stuck on the walls. My mom thought it was disgusting, but I thought it was super cool. My parents took us to Morro Bay. I didn't think it was very fun (because you couldn't climb the rock).

Mission San Antonio de Padua
Jolon, California
We spent 2½ hours – Allow 2 to 3 hours

You can do this mission and another in one day. San Miguel, for instance. That's what we did. This mission is on a military base. Tell your parents to be aware of the speed limits!

Mission San Miguel Arcangel
San Miguel, California
We spent 1¼ hours – Allow 1 to 2½ hours

Like at Mission San Luis Obispo, the church was off-limits. It was being restored. If it is completed by the time you visit, you should allow more time. We did Mission San Antonio on the same day that we did this one. At the end of the day, we played on Moonstone Beach again.

We left Cambria and traveled to Santa Barbara for a couple of days. We picked up the Lompoc and Solvang missions along the way.

Mission La Purisima Concepcion
Lompoc, California
We spent 2¼ hours – Allow 2 to 4 hours

This mission is large, and could require a lot of time. But, you can still tour it with another smaller mission. Since we did Mission Santa Ines on the same day, we didn't do any other activities in Lompoc.

Mission Santa Ines
Solvang, California
We spent 1¼ hours – Allow 1 to 2 hours

This is one of the smaller missions, and you can do it on one day, along with another mission. No activities here, either.

Mission Santa Barbara
Santa Barbara, California
We spent 1½ hours – Allow 1½ to 2½ hours

Mission Santa Barbara is medium–sized. You could probably tour it with another mission, but we didn't do that. After leaving the mission, we took a trolley tour of the city which you can catch right at the mission. I recommend it. On the tour we saw a big tree that was really awesome. We also played, ate and shopped some at Stearns Wharf. We went to a really great hands-on marine education facility called the Ty Warner Sea Center. The city courthouse was another fantastic sight. It was really pretty, and we climbed the stairs or took the elevator (I forgot which one) to the top, where we got a spectacular view of Santa Barbara.

Salinas Trip

Salinas is a good location to stay, because you are close to Mission Soledad, Mission San Juan Bautista, Mission Santa Cruz, and Mission San Carlos.

Mission Nuestra Senora de la Soledad
Soledad, California
We spent 1¼ - Allow 1 to 2 hours

You can easily tour another mission after or before doing this one. We spent the previous night in Lost Hills to shorten our journey.

Mission San Juan Bautista
San Juan Bautista, California
We spent 1½ hours – Allow 1½ to 3 hours

When our tour here was over, we went back to Salinas, to see some cool statues of gigantic hats in a park. We also went to the Steinbeck museum. It was very fun, which I find sort of surprising because I don't understand Steinbeck's stories.

Mission Santa Cruz
Santa Cruz, California
We spent 1¼ hours – Allow 1 to 2 hours

Mission Santa Cruz is a small mission, because it is a replica of the original one. Also, don't forget to visit the State Historic Park down the street. Now, **MAKE SURE YOU GO TO THE SANTA CRUZ BOARDWALK!** They have the most stupendous rollercoasters and thrill rides. You need to go there!!!!!!!!!!

Mission San Carlos Borromeo
Carmel, California
We spent 2 hours – Allow 2 to 3 hours

This is a semi–large mission. Since the city of Monterey is close, you might want to consider visiting the Monterey Bay aquarium. It's awesome!

San Francisco Trip

*S*an Francisco is a good location to stay, because you are close to two missions to the north, and two missions to the south. You have one mission in San Francisco, and tons of things to do in San Francisco. Here are some suggestions.

First, find the **concrete slides** at Seward and Douglass Streets and go down them. Bring a piece of cardboard along to go down them. Go to **Fort Point** and see the waves break. Bike the **Golden Gate Bridge**. If you want, take a ship to **Alcatraz**. Only the nighttime tour has a tour guide, and the tour guide is only with you about 20% of the time. The other 80% is with an audio thing, and it can be sort of confusing. I thought Alcatraz was just ok. Also, if you're a book fanatic like me, go to **City Lights Bookstore**. They only have a few shelves of Young Adult, but I still loved it. Go to **Ripley's Believe it or Not!** They have the coolest hands-on exhibits, and there's some stuff that's really… hard to believe. It is so fun! If you like this, go to **Exploratorium**, where there are lots more hands-on exhibits. But, my mom says it's like A.D.D. (Attention Deficit Disorder) world, because we kids want to do everything, and there's a lot of stuff there…so much stuff we didn't get to do it all in the 5 hours we were there! If your amount of time is limited at Exploratorium, only go up to the 2nd floor to do the gravel path; everything else on floor 2 is a drag. There's enough stuff on the first floor, anyway. At the end of the museum, there is the **Tactile Dome**, which is a really fun dome that is totally dark inside, and you have to find your way out. There are slides and rope ladders, and weird furry things that I don't want to know what they are. Plus, before going into the Tactile Dome, talk to Daisy. She is a computer that cannot talk, but type. You type something in, and she responds. Here is an example.

You: Hi, Daisy. How does it feel do be a computer?
Daisy: (this magically appears) How does it feel to be a human?

Daisy does not always respond to you directly. Sometimes she copies you, and sometimes she says random words that make no sense. Anyway, she is fun! Also, you will want to drive, or walk, down the most crooked street in San Francisco, **Lombard Street**. Ride the **elevator** at the Union Square **Westin Hotel**, but not if you are afraid of heights. **Sail under** the **Golden Gate Bridge**. Go to **Musee Mecanique** (bring lots of quarters). Take a tour of **Chinatown**. Make your own pizza at **Gorgio's Pizzeria**. Do this during kids' happy hour on Wednesday nights. Bark with the **sea lions** at **Pier 39**, and if you want to take a lot of public transportation, try the **cable cars**, **street cars**, **Muni Metro**, and **BART**. There are lots more things to do in San Francisco, but I can't list them all. I had a great time in San Francisco and I hope you do too.

Mission San Francisco de Solano
Sonoma, California
We spent 1¼ hours – Allow 1 to 2 hours

You may want to add a bit more time if you choose to watch the entire movie. Since we did this mission on the same day as we did Mission San Rafael, we didn't do anything in Sonoma. But my brother, a train fanatic, went to the Sonoma Train Town while we toured the mission. It was pretty fun for him there, but I don't recommend it for children above age 7. There are a lot of little-kid rides that smaller children would enjoy riding.

Mission San Rafael
San Rafael, California
We spent 1¼ hours – Allow 1 to 2 hours

Mission San Rafael is quite small. We didn't do any activities here, unless going to a Cold Stone ice cream across the street would count.

Mission San Francisco de Asis
San Francisco, California
We spent 2 hours – Allow 1½ to 2½ hours

Touring the mission itself doesn't take that long, but touring San Francisco? Days! If you want to see the things I recommend in San Fran, look at the first two pages of the San Francisco Trip.

The following two missions could easily be visited from San Francisco. We happened to stay in Morgan Hill, so we could spend the day at Gilroy Gardens amusement park and also be close to the two south bay missions. Gilroy Gardens is more of a smaller child amusement park, but I think older siblings would still enjoy riding rides with their younger brothers or sisters.

Mission Santa Clara de Asis
Santa Clara, California
We spent 2¼ hours – Allow 1½ to 2½ hours

We did this mission on the same day as San Jose, so no activities.

Mission San Jose
Fremont, California
We spent 1½ hours – Allow 1½ to 2 hours

This mission can easily be done with another mission. Mission Santa Clara, for instance. We didn't do anything else here, unless you count driving to San Mateo to see the wooden church. That should take about an additional ¾ hour.

About the Author

*T*orrey Mahall was born in Riverside, California, which is where she still lives. Her hobbies include reading, playing with her brother, reading, doing gymnastics, reading, playing piano, and reading. She was ten years old when she wrote this book, and has no pets…but hopes for a cat that she can name Toulouse. She has a slight interest in drama and acting, but wants to be a paleontologist when she grows up, with a side job as an author.

Places she likes to visit include Disneyland, Knott's Berry Farm, the Santa Cruz Boardwalk, Six Flags Magic Mountain, and Disneyworld (even though she's yet to visit the last two.) Other than amusement parks, she likes school, Barnes and Noble, Borders, going over to her friends' houses, her house, and last but certainly not least, the missions.

For more information on Torrey, please visit www.torreymahall.com. (Just kidding! There's no website. Sorry! ☹)

Update:
Since her book was published, there have been a few changes. On August 16, 2009 she got to visit Six Flags Magic Mountain. On November 18, 2009 she got to visit the four Disney World parks.

And now, there really is a place for more information on Torrey and her book. In January of 2010, she launched her website www.torreymahall.com. (Not kidding now!)

Acknowledgements

*F*irst, I would like to thank my dad for taking me to all the missions. He let me use his laptop when I was writing the stories on the road. And, he worked on getting my book published, and he helped me with my project. Thank you, Dada!

Second, I want to thank my mom for reading over my work, and telling me what I needed to fix. She also visited the missions with me. Thank you, Mama!

Third, I would like to thank my younger brother for being sort of quiet when I wrote the book. The quietest he was happened when he was taking naps in the van. He seemed to enjoy the missions he went to, and he wasn't too much of a bother there. So, thank you Jonathan!

And, I would like to thank everyone who took the time to read and review my book before having it published. I received lots of helpful feedback and encouragement from them. Their input often resulted in positive changes to my book.

Once again, thank you everyone for helping me. Or in Jonathan's case, being silent. I really appreciate it. Thanks a lot!

Bibliography

California Missions with Huell Howser (a DVD)
San Diego de Alcala: California's First Mission
    by I. Brent Eagen
Mission San Carlos Borromeo by unknown author
Padres and People of Old Mission San Antonio
    by Beatrice Casey
Mission San Gabriel Arcangel by unknown author
Mission San Luis Obispo de Tolosa
    by Joseph A. Carotenuti and Tim Olson
Mission San Francisco de Asis by Mary Null Boule
Mission San Juan Capistrano by unknown author
Mission San Juan Capistrano by Kathleen J. Edgar
    and Susan E. Edgar
Mission San Juan Capistrano map and guide
    by The Mission San Juan Capistrano Docent Society
Mission Santa Clara de Asis by Mary Null Boule
Mission San Buenaventura by Mary Null Boule
Mission Santa Barbara based on the text
    by Maynard Geiger O.F.M., Ph. D
The Living History of La Purisima Mission
    by The Lompoc Record
Mission La Purisima Concepcion by Mary Null Boule
Mission Santa Cruz by Mary Null Boule
Mission Nuestra Senora de la Soledad by Mary Null Boule
Mission San Jose by Mary Null Boule
Mission San Juan Bautista by Lowman Publishing
California's Mission San Miguel Arcangel
    by Franciscan Padres
San Fernando Rey de Espana Mission
    by Msgr. Francis J. Weber
Mission San Luis Rey: A Pocket History by Harry Kelsey
Mission Santa Ines: The Hidden Gem by Cresencia
    and Dale Olmstead Photography by Jim Frank
Mission San Rafael Arcangel by Mary Null Boule

Mission San Francisco Solano by Mary Null Boule
Harry Downie www.carmelmission.org
Martin de Porres en.wikipedia.org
San Francisco Genealogy www.sfgenealogy.com
San Francisco Cemeteries www.sanfranciscocemeteries.com
Saint Francis and the wolf from www.tamingthewolf.com
El Camino Real (California) from en.wikipedia.org
El Camino Real Bell from www.hmdb.org
El Camino Real Bell Marker Project from www.dot.ca.gov
El Camino Real, California's Coast Route
    www.americanroads.us/autotrails/elcaminoreal.html
Basilica from en.wikipedia.org
Basilicas of the United States from www.catholichistory.net
Basilica from www.absoluteastronomy.com
What is a Basilica? from www.wisegeek.com
California Mission Nicknames from www.serraschool.org and
    missiontour.org
Brochures from the various missions

www.ingramcontent.com/pod-product-compliance
Lightning Source LLC
LaVergne TN
LVHW021713060526
838200LV00050B/2639